HANDBOOK OF EXTERIOR HOME REPAIRS: A PRACTICAL ILLUSTRATED GUIDE

ALSO BY THE AUTHOR

The New Homeowner's Illustrated Handbook: A
Do-It-Yourself Repair Guide to Problems
That Are Sure to Occur

HANDBOOK OF EXTERIOR HOME REPAIRS: A PRACTICAL ILLUSTRATED GUIDE

Herbert F. Holtje

ILLUSTRATIONS BY
Adrienne Holtje

Parker Publishing Company, Inc.
West Nyack, New York

© 1979 by

PARKER PUBLISHING COMPANY, INC.

West Nyack, New York

643.7
H758

Library of Congress Cataloging in Publication Data

Holtje, Herbert
   Handbook of exterior home repairs.

   Includes index.
   1. Dwellings—Maintenance and repair—Amateurs'
manuals. I. Holtje, Adrienne. II. Title.
TH4817.3.H64   643'.7   79-12414
ISBN 0-13-377655-7

Printed in the United States of America

There is Only One Book
Devoted Entirely to Saving You Time
and Money on Your
Exterior Home Repairs . . . . and This is it.

Whether you live in a warm, sunny climate, or in a cold and damp part of the country, the outside of your house is under constant attack by nature and pollution. Even an ordinary oil burner can deposit a paint-destroying layer of soot on a house in a single heating season. A few drops of frozen water can split concrete, and undetected fungus can ruin a brand new paint job. Is it any wonder that some of the most expensive repairs must be made to the outside of a house?

But why pay through the nose to have others do work that you can do yourself? The chances are that you will be able to handle most of the repairs better than many of the so-called professionals and that you will be able to save considerable money in the bargain. When you think about it, there is no better way to protect your real estate investment than by keeping the exterior of your house in good shape.

The solutions to exterior problems are not always included in general home repair books. Therefore, this book is filled with nothing but money-saving ways to solve these problems. It's *the* "specialist" in a field of general how-to books, and the only book you'll ever need to do most of your own exterior repair work.

This book is more than just a collection of solutions to exterior problems. It's a guide to understanding the problems, and a source of early-warning signals to make sure that little problems don't turn into big expensive ones.

HERE ARE SOME SPECIFIC WAYS
THIS BOOK WILL HELP YOU

- When you use the professional check list in Chapter 1, you will be able to spot little problems that often can be fixed in minutes at little or no cost. If neglected for even a few months, some of the problems could cost thousands of dollars to fix.

- You will learn how to make simple roof repairs that, if neglected, can cause thousands of dollars worth of damage inside as well as outside the house.

- Using an extension ladder is easy, but unless you know and use the tricks outlined in this book you can further damage your house and seriously hurt yourself.

- Many people have spent thousands of dollars to fix and waterproof a basement, when all that may have been needed was a relocation of the downspout. Find out how you can solve this big problem with a simple solution.

- You can work just as hard caulking a joint with one compound as with another. But do you know which material is best for each job? If you don't, a simple leaky joint can result in the need for extensive and expensive repairs. Find out which caulking you should use in Chapter 5.

- Have you ever priced the professional repair of a small hole in a stucco wall? How about a big one? You will save at least ten times the cost of this book when you learn to do this job yourself.

- Do you know that mildew can grow under a layer of freshly applied paint, and destroy it in months? And this can happen even on the sunny side of the house! When it costs several thousand dollars to paint an average-size house, you should know how to prevent mildew. Chapter 5 tells the whole story.

- Water paint or oil paint? Most paint stores will sell you the paint that they make the greatest profit on, so you should be prepared to make the right decision before you enter the shop. You can learn which is the right paint for your house in Chapter 6.

- Beware of bargain brushes. Not only do they have a short life, they will give you all kinds of problems while you are painting. Learn how to select the right brush in Chapter 6.
- The paint selection guide in Chapter 6 is worth the price of the book alone. When you use it, you will never have to wonder which is the right paint for a particular surface.
- When a window rattles, it can do more than annoy you; it can let valuable heat escape and cost you considerable money in higher fuel bills. Learn how to seal every type of window used in home construction in Chapter 7.
- Learn how to replace glass and repair screening—two simple jobs that can make home-repair services rich.
- If your locks are faulty, you invite a burglar. In Chapter 8 you will learn how to keep your house safe and secure.
- Steps, walks, walls and driveways have many ways of making problems that are not only annoying, but can be dangerous and even cause expensive law suits. Everything you need to know to solve these problems will be found in Chapter 9.
- And this is only a small sample. See the table of contents for a listing of all the professional repairs that you can do.

If you visualize everything that is exposed to nature, it's easy to see why you need this book. Paint, roofing, gutters, masonry, chimneys, siding, plastic, glass, wood, metal and many other materials are slowly being eroded, dulled, worn, rotted, chipped and broken. This book was written to help you overcome these problems yourself, inexpensively and professionally.

7

CONTENTS

Introduction   5

**CHAPTER 1 – HOW TO GET THE JUMP ON
EXTERIOR PROBLEMS—
USE THIS PROFESSIONAL
CHECKLIST   13**

Safety—Safety—Safety (22)

CHAPTER 2 – HOW TO FIX ANY ROOF   25

How To Use an Extension Ladder (27)
Climbing a Ladder (30) How to Spot
Leaks (31) How to Repair Asphalt Shin-
gles (33) How to Replace Asphalt Shin-
gles (34) How to Repair a Hip Shingle (36)
How to Replace a Hip Shingle (37) How to
Repair a Damaged Slate (38) How to Re-
place a Slate Shingle (38) How to Apply As-
phalt Paint to a Flat Roof (39) How to Patch
a Flat Roof (40) How to Repair Wood
Shingles (44) How to Replace a Wood Shin-
gle (45) How to Repair Ceramic Tile
Roofs (45) How to Repair Flashing (48)
How to Replace Flashing on a Vent
Pipe (49) How to Repair Open and Closed
Valley Flashing (51) Other Flashing Prob-
lems (53) How to Fix a Leak Around a
Skylight (53) Some Common Roof-Patching
Materials (54)

9

CHAPTER 3 – HOW TO REPAIR GUTTERS AND DOWNSPOUTS   55

How to Clean Gutters and Downspouts (58) How to Install Leaf Guards and Strainers (59) How to Fix a Sagging Gutter (61) How to Patch a Small Hole in a Metal Gutter (63) How to Patch a Large Hole in a Metal Gutter (66) How to Preserve Wood Gutters (66) How to Care For Steel Gutters (67) How to Care for Copper Gutters (68) How to Care for Aluminum Gutters (68) How to Care for Plastic Gutters (69) How to Install Aluminum Gutters (69) How to Install Splashblocks (71) How to Install a Dry Well (72) Snow Guards (74)

CHAPTER 4 – CARING FOR YOUR CHIMNEY   75

How to Clean a Chimney (78) How to Install a Spark Arrester (81) How to Keep Rain out of Your Chimney (82) How to Repair Flashing (83) How to Replace Flashing on a Chimney (85) What to do About a Leaning Chimney (89) What to Do If You See Smoke Coming from Between Bricks (89) How to Replace Chimney Mortar (90) How to Replace Loose Chimney Bricks (91) How to Repair a Chimney Cap (92) Fireplace Problems (93)

CHAPTER 5 – THE CARE AND REPAIR OF SIDING   95

How to Caulk Exterior Joints (97) How to Prepare a Surface for Caulking (102) How to Strengthen Warped Clapboard (104) How to Repair Split Clapboard (104) How

**CHAPTER 5 – THE CARE AND REPAIR
OF SIDING (continued)**

to Replace a Section of Clapboard (106)
How to Strengthen a Warped Wood
Shingle (108) How to Replace Damaged
Wood Shingle (109) How to Replace As-
bestos Shingles (110) How to Mix
Stucco (111) How to Patch Small Cracks in
Stucco (111) How to Patch Large Holes in
Stucco Over a Wood Frame (112) How to
Patch a Hole in Stucco Over a Concrete
Block Wall (113) How to Repair Brick
Work (114) How to Solve Problems of Mil-
dew (114)

**CHAPTER 6 – HOW TO PAINT AND PRESERVE
EXTERIOR SURFACES   117**

How to Spot all Paint Problems (119) How
to Prepare an Exterior Surface for Paint-
ing (120) How to Choose the Right
Brush (132) How to Care for Your
Brushes (134) Here's What Paint You
Should Use (137) Here's the Order in Which
to Paint the Outside of Your House (139)
How to Apply Paint to Siding (140) How to
Paint Everything Else Outside the
House (140)

**CHAPTER 7 – HOW TO FIX ANYTHING
THAT CAN GO WRONG WITH
WINDOWS, SCREENS
AND STORM WINDOWS   143**

The Double-Hung Window (146) The
Casement Window (163) Storm Win-
dows (166) Jalousie Windows (170) Awning
Windows (172) Screens (172)

**CHAPTER 8 – HOW TO FIX DOORS
AND LOCKS**   **179**

How to Repair a Worn Screw Hole (182)
How to Shim a Hinge (183) How to Deepen
a Hinge Mortise (184) How to Remove a
Door (185) How To Fix a Sticking
Door (186) How to Fix a Door That Will
Not Latch (189) How to Correct a Warped
Door (191) How to Replace a Saddle (193)
How to Install a Peephole (195) How to In-
stall Weatherstripping (196) How to Fix
Sliding Doors (200) How to Fix Lock Prob-
lems (202) How to Solve Garage Door
Problems (211)

**CHAPTER 9 – HOW TO FIX STEPS,
WALKS, WALLS AND
DRIVEWAYS**   **215**

How to Mix Mortar (218) How to Color
Mortar (219) How to Use Mortar (220) How
to Use a Trowel (220) How to Cure Concrete (221) How to Repoint Brick (222)
How to Fix Large Cracks Caused by Settling (224) How to Replace Damaged
Brick (227) How to Handle the Problem of
Efflorescence (228) How to Repair Damaged Concrete Walls (229) How to Repair a
Damaged Concrete Step (230) How to Seal
a Blacktop Driveway (232) How to Patch
Cracks in Blacktop (233) How to Fill a Hole
in Blacktop (234)

Index   237

HOW TO
GET THE JUMP ON
EXTERIOR PROBLEMS—
USE THIS
PROFESSIONAL
INSPECTION CHECK LIST

If you wait until you have problems, the repairs may be difficult and expensive. But, if you take the time to make a routine inspection of the exterior of your house, you can often spot problems-in-the-making. For example, blistered paint may mean that there is water in the wood which is working its way out. How did it get there? How much has already gotten in, and has it done any damage besides lifting the paint? Little blisters themselves are relatively easy to remedy, but unless you find out how the water got behind the paint, you could have some very serious problems later.

It isn't necessary to become a slave to your house. An occasional walk-around observation will often do, but more important is the knowledge of what to look for. Knowing the symptoms, you will be able to spot problems and to fix them before they get out of hand.

One man who knew the symptoms to look for spotted some blistering paint while sunning himself in his backyard. He wasn't looking for trouble, but as his eye wandered over the siding, he saw the problem. Upon closer inspection, he found that a fresh paint job had begun to peel in one spot. He knew he would have to resurface the area, but because he understood that water from behind shingles can cause blisters, he was able to find and repair some damaged flashing that could have caused over a thousand dollars worth of damages if it had gone undetected.

Rather than give you a rigid list, I have arranged the most important symptoms in the order in which their solu-

15

tions appear in this book. Not all symptoms will be as meaningful to everyone. For example, if you live in a part of the country that is normally cool and dry, the problem of mildew may not be terribly important. After an occasional damp spell, any mildew you have may simply disappear. But, if you live in an area that is plagued by warm temperatures and high humidity, mildew can do serious damage. These problems, and their relative importance have been pointed out in each chapter, and you should evaluate the symptoms and problems as they relate to your specific location and conditions.

It has been estimated that more than half the costs of major home repairs can be either eliminated, or at least drastically reduced if the problems are solved when they first occur. Most problems get worse gradually, and it is difficult to tell from one day to the next just what is happening. If you could leave your house and return six months or a year later, you would notice some very decided changes. But, living in the house, it is difficult to notice changes day by day.

Some changes occur rather abruptly. If you don't spot them you can have problems immediately. A crack that appears in a brick wall indicates that there are other problems, such as shifting, but much of the problem has already taken place by the time the crack appears.

The point is this—unless you train your eye to spot the changes, and unless you make regular inspections of the critical parts of the exterior of your house, you could end up with serious problems and expensive repair bills.

In the pages that follow, I am going to describe what you should look for when you make your inspection. This is not a check list that should be followed slavishly. Rather, it is a description of problems that can occur. From this you can make up your own check list, depending on your location and the materials used in the construction of your house.

Of course, much of the inspection can be done on an informal basis. That is, you can give your paint the once-over as you water the lawn. There is no waste of time and effort in this. You can check the condition of your roof when you trim nearby trees. You can even get an idea of the condition of a porch roof when you look out of an upstairs window to see if it's going to rain on your picnic.

If you are able to get yourself into this kind of thinking, there will be little need for a rigid inspection. Your eye will simply go to the areas where problems can occur as you are doing different things about the house and you'll note where there has been a change, and whether or not it's time to do something about it.

Before a pilot takes up a plane, whether he is flying a single seat tail-dragger, or a multi-engine jet transport, it is standard operating procedure to make a thorough ground check of the equipment. A walk around the plane, a tug of the flywires and an inspection of every part that is visible that could have problems is very important. A house represents a substantial investment—the largest sum most people spend on a single item in a lifetime. So, why not decide right now that you are going to protect that investment. Decide to make a note of the points to check that refer to your house and keep them in mind every time you are outside.

Here's the list. It's organized by the topics covered in this book—by chapter.

Chapter 2 – The Roof

1. Watch for branches that fall on the roof from nearby trees. They can punch holes, rip shingles, split slate and do structural damage to the supporting frame.

2. Make a regular inspection of the underside of your roof during a rainstorm. The only way you'll know if there are any leaks is to check when there is water on the roof.

3. If you notice water spots on walls and inside ceilings, follow the instructions for locating the leaks described in Chapter 2.

4. Inspect the roof for loose, worn, torn and broken shingles. If you can, look at the roof during a

windstorm—from the ground. Note whether any shingles lift in the wind.

5. Inspect the peaks and valleys. Look for broken shingles on the peaks, and damaged flashing in the valleys.

6. Look for holes on a rolled asphalt roof. Watch for signs of severe weathering. Look for blisters and damage caused by nearby or fallen tree branches.

7. Look for wind-lifted, warped and cracked wood shingles.

8. Inspect the flashing wherever it has been used. Look at areas around vent pipes and the flashing that has been applied around a chimney. Check the caulking on the chimney flashing.

Chapter 3 – Gutters and Downspouts

1. Check for clogged gutters and downspouts. If your house is near deciduous trees, it may be necessary to clean leaves from the gutters at least twice a year.

2. Check the facia board and roof overhang for signs of rot.

3. Check to make sure that whatever finish was used—paint, oil, stain, etc.—is intact.

4. Determine if you would benefit from leaf guards and downspout strainers.

5. Look for a sagging gutter. A gutter should have a slight pitch to carry the water to the downspout, but if it sags out of shape, the water can collect and overflow before it ever reaches the downspout.

6. Check your gutters for holes.

7. Check to see if the run-off from the downspout is eroding the ground. Install splashblocks, a drain tile, or another system to carry the water away from the house.

8. Check during a period of heavy snow to see if sliding snow is doing any damage to your gutters. Snow guards may be needed.

Chapter 4 – Chimneys

1. Inspect the flue lining of your chimney. If it is used regularly, every few months is appropriate. Look for a build-up of soot and an accumulation of debris blown in from the outside. If the chimney is used infrequently, look for bird and squirrel nests before you build a fire in the fireplace.

2. Watch the top of your chimney while you have a fire in the fireplace. Do this at night so you can see if there are a lot of sparks issuing from the flue. A spark arrester may be needed.

3. Check your fireplace during a heavy rainstorm. You may have to install a rain cap.

4. Check the chimney flashing carefully.

5. See if your chimney is leaning away from the true center.

6. Check to see if the mortar between the bricks is drying and crumbling away.

7. Check for loose bricks.

8. Inspect the chimney cap for crumbling mortar.

9. Inspect the masonry and the mortar in the fireplace.

Chapter 5 – Siding

1. Inspect all joints for dried and cracking caulking. See Chapter 5 for a list of specific check points.

2. Check clapboard for warping and cracks.

3. Check for warped and damaged wood shingles.

4. Check for cracked asbestos shingles.

5. Look for cracks and holes in stucco.

6. Check for cracks in brick facing.
7. Inspect for mildew.

Chapter 6 – Exterior Surface Finishes

1. Inspect all painted surfaces for the following: Blisters, peeling, chalking, checking and alligatoring, cracking and scaling, discoloration, moss and efflorescence.
2. Look for discoloration caused by nailheads.
3. Loof for caulking.
4. Check gutters for the condition of the surface.
5. Check the surface of porches and decks.

Chapter 7 – Windows, Screens and Storm Windows

1. Inspect the frame and stops on double-hung windows for binding.
2. Inspect for cracked glass.
3. Inspect the condition of the sash cord, if it is made of rope.
4. Inspect the condition of the spring-lift window devices for proper adjustment.
5. Inspect the condition of the putty.
6. Check for air leaks.
7. Check the lubrication of casement window actuators and hinges.
8. Inspect for condensation.
9. Check the seal of storm windows.
10. Check the glass and operating mechanism in jalousie windows.
11. Inspect screens for holes.
12. Check the condition of screen and storm window frames.

Chapter 8 – Doors and Locks

1. Check to make sure that all door hinges are firmly screwed in place.
2. Check to make sure that the door doesn't bind in the frame.
3. Check to make sure the door latches securely.
4. See if any of your doors are warping.
5. Check for air leaks. Check weatherstripping if it has been installed.
6. Check the action of sliding doors.
7. Check the mounting of a rail-hung door.
8. Make sure that all the keys for all locks work.
9. Check to see if a lock is sticky and difficult to turn.
10. Check the track mounts and wheels on overhead garage doors.

Chapter 9 – Walks, Walls and Driveways

1. Check the condition of mortar between bricks.
2. Look for cracks in masonry walls.
3. Check for damaged and loose bricks.
4. Look for efflorescence on wall surfaces.
5. Check the condition of concrete and other types of steps.
6. Check the surface condition of a blacktop driveway.
7. Check for cracks and holes in blacktop.

There they are—the major points to check in your house. You probably noticed that some of the points were mentioned more than once. Roof gutters were included in two sections, for example. This was not an oversight. Not every house is built in the same way and of the same materials. The duplication insures that you will check every item that pertains to your own house.

Are there any times that are better than others for checking a house? The answer to this is yes, and the times are determined pretty much by the seasons. For example, after a winter, it's a good idea to look for frost damage in outside masonry, paint peeling problems, snow damage to roofs and gutters and for openings at caulked joints.

At the end of the summer, you should look for problems that could have been caused by high temperatures and rain; leaky roofs, for example, and such troubles as gutters plugged with leaves, and problems with wood siding.

In the spring, if you look up and see green leaves sprouting from your gutters, you will know that you forgot to clean them in the fall. The accumulated debris has provided a seed bed for what the wind brings—I have seen small maple trees sprouting from gutters in my home town.

Don't become a slave to this check list but, whatever you do, don't make it just an annual affair. If severe weather conditions in your area have more of an effect on certain parts of the house, adjust your inspection accordingly. Be on the lookout all the time. Keeping an eye on your house can save you a lot of time and money.

SAFETY — SAFETY — SAFETY

Many of the repairs described in this book require that you take certain safety precautions. None of the repairs themselves are particularly dangerous, except possibly climbing on a roof. But it is important to note here—before you undertake any of the repairs—that you use certain precautions.

For example, whenever you are chipping brick, mortar and any dry masonry, chips will fly. You need more than safety glasses for this job—you need safety goggles. Goggles cover your eyes completely and no flying particles can get behind them.

Cutting wood and doing many of the siding repairs can

also send chips flying. Be sure to protect your eyes when you solve these problems.

Paint and some of the cleaners and solvents mentioned in this book are harmful, especially if you get them in your eyes. Some people have allergic reactions to some of the materials, and most of them should be used in open spaces where there are no concentrated fumes to breathe.

When dealing with exterior home repair, you will be doing a lot of climbing around your house. This can be dangerous if you are not careful. To reduce problems here, I have included some very specific instructions on the use of a ladder in the beginning of Chapter 2.

Tools themselves can be dangerous if you are unfamiliar with their use. This can be an especially serious problem if you are on a roof for the first time and are just learning how to swing a hammer or use a saw. I strongly urge you to make some practice cuts and swings on the ground before you take your tools aloft.

In most cases, just plain common sense will prevail, and you should have no problems. But, if you are doing a repair for the first time with an unfamiliar tool, know the safety precautions to use with the tool and practice first.

2

HOW TO
FIX
ANY ROOF

Apart from such obvious problems as holes made by fallen branches, most of the work required to keep a roof in shape involves locating and sealing leaks. Replacing a shingle, sealing cracks and fixing flashing are all jobs that most homeowners will face sooner or later, and this chapter tells how to handle these and all the others that can occur. However, before any of the actual repair is undertaken, you should be very familiar with the use of an extension ladder and know the tricks of locating leaks. Don't be surprised if a water spot on a second floor ceiling is caused by a roof leak on the opposite side of the house.

HOW TO USE AN EXTENSION LADDER

There is more to using an extension ladder than simply propping it against the house—that is, if you want to keep from breaking bones and windows. Extension ladders are made in different lengths, but all of them are constructed so that one section telescopes from the other, and can be lifted by using the integral rope and pulley.

The story is told of a man who moved to the suburbs, bought an extension ladder, and planned to save himslf a lot of money by doing his own exterior painting. He just might have done it if he had taken the time to learn how to use his ladder. Rather, he figured all that was necessary was to lean it against the house and go to work. Unfortunately, he extended it all the way, but only planted it a few feet away from the foundation. When he got to the top, his weight was past the center, and the ladder swung out. By the time he figured his hospital bills, time away from work and the cost to have the job done by a professional painter, he lost, rather than saved, many thousands of dollars.

Always begin with the extension ladder fully closed, and place the foot of the ladder in position against the foundation. This means that the pulley will be at the end of the ladder farthest from the house.

With the foot of the ladder firmly braced where the ground meets the foundation, "walk" the ladder up from the pulley end. When the ladder is fully vertical and parallel with the side of the house, lift the base slightly and move it outward so that it will be leaning on the house. Watch out for windows.

Now, raise the telescoping section by pulling down on the lifting rope. This will require a little practice—moving the ladder away from the house slightly, balancing it and tugging on the lifting rope at the same time. Don't try to lift too much of the extension section at one time. It is better to lift the ladder one rung at a time until you feel comfortable handling it.

As the ladder is lifted, there are hooks on the lower section of the extension portion that will latch on to successive rungs of the base section as it is lifted. When you have reached the area of the house where you will be working, the ladder will latch safely in place. However, it is a good idea to secure the loose end of the lifting rope to a lower rung of the base section to keep it from tripping you as you walk around the base of the ladder or as you climb it.

Lowering an extension ladder is simply a matter of using the lifting rope to pull the extension section up over the rung on the base section which held the ladder and then slowly lowering the section. There are catches which will be tripped when this is done to permit the ladder to be lowered. Always store an extension ladder in the fully lowered position and lash the rope safely out of the way.

2-1-A
Place the base of the ladder firmly against the foundation
of the house, and "walk" it up to position.

2-1-B
Pull the base on the ladder away from the base of the house
a distance equivalent to one fourth of the extended length
of the ladder.

CLIMBING A LADDER

Before you climb a ladder, make sure that the distance from the base of the ladder to the wall on which it is leaning is about one-fourth the length of the ladder as it is extended. When a ladder is set too steeply, it can tumble backward when you reach the top; a ladder set too far away from the base of the wall can break as you reach the middle.

Climb with your body close to the frame of the ladder, but be sure that your arms are free to move. You should use both arms; don't try to carry anything as you climb. Tools can

2-2
To be safe, keep your hips within the sides of the ladder and never stretch to the point where your hips leave this position. Don't work with two hands; use one hand to hold on and the other to work.

be tucked in pockets, or hauled up with a line you carry in a pocket. If you are tempted to extend your reach to either side of the ladder, a safe rule to follow is to always keep your hips within the ladder rails.

If you are going to climb off the ladder onto a roof, make sure that the ladder extends beyond the edge so that you can step off. Don't try to climb up from a low ladder; getting on the roof seldom presents problems, but you will find it tricky getting back down when your work is finished.

If you are going to be working on a steep roof, the safest thing to do is to make the ladder attachment shown. You will not only be a lot safer, you will also be able to work more quickly without having to spend a lot of effort holding on.

HOW TO SPOT LEAKS

Before you can fix a leak, you have to find it, and this may not be an easy job. Leaking rain water has a way of running some distance from the actual hole to the point where it becomes obvious. If the underside of your roof is accessible you should have no problems. But, if you have a finished ceiling or insulation under the roof, there is seldom an alternative to the removal of the material to locate the leak.

Holes can often be spotted from the inside of a dark attic on a bright, sunny day, but rain leaks usually call for immediate attention.

Begin the search by locating the point where the water was noticed, on the ceiling below for example. Then, try to trace its flow to the point where it has entered through the roof. This can often be quite a distance, and many leaks are found at the flashing around vents and chimneys. If the flashing was not copper, it could have corroded and admitted water, or the sealing compound at the joint could have dried out and cracked open.

Peaks and valleys on the roof are the next most likely places to find leaks. Water can collect in a valley to cause rot and the leak. At peaks, erosion and cracking can cause leaks

2-3
The water you see in a room may have traveled a long
distance from where it entered through the roof.

easily. It is also possible for a break in the surface of the roof
or the underlayer to take place. Shingles can be lifted by
the wind and helped to stay up by wind-driven debris. This
can expose the nailheads holding the next course of shingles
and lead to a leak.

Whatever the source of the leak, the next step is often an
emergency one—stop the leak until the rain stops and the roof
dries so that repairs can be handled. When the leak has been
found, mark it with a crayon so that it can be located when the
repair is to be tackled. If the leak is serious and the water
must be stopped immediately, pack some caulking material or
putty into the hole until the weather clears.

These repairs are all made from the outside of the roof, but the leaks must be located from the inside. Unless you have a good eye, spotting the leak outside once it has been marked inside will be next to impossible. However, you can save yourself a lot of trouble by driving a nail up through the leak from the underside of the roof to the outside. When you are ready to make the repair, it is a simple matter to spot the nail. If this is done, and it will be a while before the repair can be made, it is wise to pack some caulking compound over the head of the nail and into the leak.

Once you are sure of the source of the leak, you are ready to handle the repair.

HOW TO REPAIR ASPHALT SHINGLES

Shingles can bend, lift, curl and rip, but all of these problems are easy to solve if the damage is not extensive. Lifted and curled shingles can be fixed by coating the bottom with some roofing cement and pressing the shingle back in place. This job should be done in the warm weather when the asphalt material is pliable and won't crack. If you can't wait for warm weather, use a hair drier, an ordinary clothes iron or a torch to do the job. Obviously, if you use a propane torch, be careful not to start a fire.

A torn shingle can be repaired in much the same way. However, after the underside of the torn sections have been coated with roofing cement and pressed in place, both sides should be nailed down with roofing nails. A single nail on either side of the tear should be sufficient. However, the heads of the nails should be coated with roofing cement and the outside of the rip should be given a coat of cement.

When a shingle tear extends beyond the area overlapped by the next course of shingles, you should slide a piece of aluminum or copper flashing well up under the crack. To get the plate up where it will offer the best protection, it may be necessary to saw through the nails that hold the shingle in place. Once the plate is in position, nail it down with several roofing nails and coat the heads with roofing cement. Then, press the portions of the torn shingle in place and coat the tear with roofing cement.

HOW TO REPLACE ASPHALT SHINGLES

When an asphalt shingle is too badly torn or curled, it should be replaced. Remember that shingles are laid on a roof overlapping from the bottom to the top. So, to get at the nails that hold the torn shingle, you will have to lift the shingle above. But, this should be done gently, and preferably on a warm day when the shingles will be pliable.

When you lift the shingle above the damaged shingle, you will see the heads of the nails that hold the shingle you plan to replace. Use a prying tool to lift the heads and the claw of a carpenter's hammer to remove the nails. If you find it impossible to lift the nails this way, use a saw blade under the

2-4-A
Lift the shingle above the damaged shingle. Use a pry bar
to remove the nails holding the damaged shingle. Be careful
not to damage the good shingle by flexing it too much.
When you work in the warm weather, asphalt shingles
will be easier to handle.

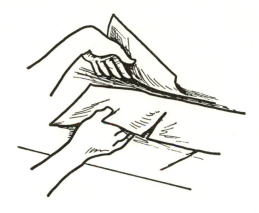

2-4-B
After the damaged shingle has been removed, slip a new
one in place. Position it to match the others.

2-4-C
Use broadhead roofing nails to nail the new shingle in place.
Apply a coat of roofing cement to the nailheads.

damaged shingle to cut through the nail shanks. If you saw
through the nails, be sure to remove the rest of the nail once
the shingle has been removed and before the new shingle is
placed in position.

Now, slide the replacement shingle in place, but be careful not to tear any of the roofing paper below the shingles. If the replacement shingle doesn't quite fit, trim the upper corners slightly and try for a fit.

Once the shingle fits snugly, it should be nailed in place. Lift the shingle above the replacement so that the nailheads will be completely covered. Cover the nailheads with a dab of roofing cement before pressing the upper shingle back in place.

HOW TO REPAIR A HIP SHINGLE

A roof peak is protected by a hip shingle—a shingle which is nailed in the same overlapping fashion as other shingles, but which is bent to the contour of the peak. Because of the stress created in the bend and the constant exposure to all kinds of weather, hip shingles often develop cracks. A cracked hip shingle in a strong wind is likely to rip partially or be blown off altogether. A careful inspection of hip shingles two or three times a year can save you lots of problems.

The repair is simple. Use enough roofing cement to hold the torn sections down. If there is a large tear, apply some cement to the outer surface of the shingle, on and around the crack.

2-5
Damaged hip roof shingles can be repaired with an
application of a roofing cement.

HOW TO REPLACE A HIP SHINGLE

Hip shingles are replaced in much the same manner as other asphalt shingles, and the replacement should have at

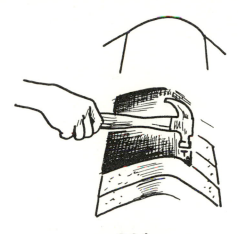

2-6-A
Allow about a 3 inch overlap when replacing a hip shingle.
Nail down at all four corners.

2-6-B
Coat the bottom of the replacement shingle with roofing cement before placing it in position. Nail down all four corners and cover the nailheads with roofing cement.

least a three-inch overlap. Before applying the replacement
shingle, nail down the bottom shingle, and cover the nailheads
with roofing cement. Brush a coat of roofing cement on the
underside of the replacement shingle before it is positioned.
Once positioned, it should be nailed down with roofing nails at
all four corners. Apply a dab of roofing cement over the exposed nailheads and the job is done.

HOW TO REPAIR A DAMAGED SLATE

When a piece of slate breaks off, but not enough stone is
lost to cause a leak, the only thing that can be done is to work
enough roofing cement over the exposed shingle to prevent
water from finding its way into the house.

HOW TO REPLACE A SLATE SHINGLE

Unlike asphalt shingles, which can be bent to accommodate tools and working hands, slate shingles are rigid. Therefore, in order to remove broken portions of a slate shingle, it
will be necessary to slip a hacksaw blade up under the remaining section to cut through all of the roofing nails that hold it in
place. Once the nails have been cut, the portions of broken
slate can be slipped out.

Be sure to have replacement slate ready before you remove the broken shards. Measure the area to be filled with
the new slate, and score the new piece deeply on both sides,
with a chisel, to the proper dimensions. Slate can be broken
easily when snapped over a straight edge on the scored lines.
Any remaining rough edges can be chipped away with a pair
of pliers or by light hammer taps.

Once the slate has been cut and you find that it fits properly, mark the position of the nail hole with a crayon. Don't
try to drive nail holes through the slate while it is in position
on the roof. Remove it and place it on an even flat surface to
make the holes. If you have acquired some skill with slate by
practicing on scrap pieces, it is possible to make the nail holes

with a hammer and a nail set. But, it is also possible to split your nicely cut replacement with a misplaced tap. The best bet is to drill the holes with an electric drill and a masonry bit.

Before the replacement slate is positioned on the roof, apply a liberal coat of roofing cement on the slate that will be covered. Then slip the new slate into position and drive roofing nails through the pre-drilled holes. Be careful that your hammer face doesn't strike the slate as the nail is driven home. You can crack the new slate at this point very easily. If you use a bell-face claw hammer, there will be little chance of this happening. This hammer has a slightly rounded face to prevent the edge from marring wood and splitting slate as the final blows are made. Don't forget to apply a dab of roofing cement over the new nailheads.

HOW TO APPLY ASPHALT PAINT
TO A FLAT ROOF

If a roof is not pitched too steeply, rolled asphalt roofing material is often applied, rather than course after course of shingles. If the entire surface has weathered, but not badly enough to need replacement, the roof will often respond well to an application of roofing paint. Black asphalt roofing paint is sold in five-gallon buckets that can cover about 500 square feet.

Before any paint is applied the roof should be swept clean and it should be dry. The paint is best applied with a long-handled brush made especially for the job. However, an old, clean push broom can be pressed into service if the special brush is not available.

Begin at the highest part of the roof and work downward by covering small areas at a time. Work the paint into the roof and be sure that you don't leave any uncovered spots. Don't be like the inside painter who paints himself into a corner; make sure you work your way toward a conveniently placed ladder.

HOW TO PATCH A FLAT ROOF

Once you have found the source of a leak or spotted a blister on roll roofing material, the repair job is relatively easy. Before beginning any repairs, sweep the area carefully.

To patch a small crack in a flat roof, first brush all debris out of the crack. Then work some roofing cement into the crack and about two inches all around it. Lay a piece of roofing felt over the cemented area and also coat that with roofing cement. Spread the roofing cement about an inch past the edges of the felt patch to complete the job.

When you spot a blister on flat roofing material, it should be repaired before it opens and becomes a leak. Look for blisters at the end of the summer and try do to the repair job while the weather is still warm and the roofing material is pliable.

2-7-A
Slice through the blistered roofing, but be careful not to cut the layer below.

2-7-B
Push enough roofing cement under both sides of the blister to seal the slice when it is pressed flat.

2-7-C
Drive flathead roofing nails around the blister.

2-7-D
Cover the nailheads and the slit with roofing cement.

2-7-E
Apply a shingle patch over the sealed blister. Use roofing
nails, and then cover the patch and the edges with another
coat of roofing cement.

Use a sharp knife to slit open the blister, but be very
careful not to cut any of the material below. Lift both sides of
the sliced blister and apply roofing cement under the blistered
area. Using roofing nails, nail down the edges around the
opening; the nails should be spaced about an inch apart. Apply

a coat of roofing cement over the cut and the nailheads and then apply a patch made of asphalt shingle material. Once the patch has been nailed in place, cover it with roofing cement. Extend the cement an inch or two beyond the edges of the patch to make sure that no rain can find its way in.

A large blister, or a badly damaged section of flat roofing material, should be replaced rather than patched. Begin by cutting out the section of damaged material. Even though the area may be quite irregular, try to remove the roofing as a rectangular piece.

Once the damaged material has been removed, brush the underlying area thoroughly and apply a coat of roofing cement. The roofing cement should be spread under the edges of the remaining roofing material. When you lift this section, be careful not to tear it.

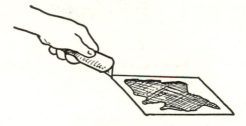

2-8-A
Use a sharp knife to cut out the damaged area
in a rectangular pattern. Be careful not to damage
the underlying material.

2-8-B
Apply a coating of roofing cement to the exposed area and to
the underside of a patch made of roofing felt.

2-8-C
Nail down the patch of roofing felt.

2-8-D
Apply a coating of roofing cement over the patch.

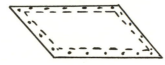

2-8-E
Make another patch, this time of shingle material. Coat the underside and place it over the felt patch. It should be an inch or two larger than the felt patch on all sides. Nail this patch in place.

2-8-F
Cover the new patch and the surrounding edges with roofing cement.

Fit a piece of roofing material cut to match the hole, and coat the patch with roofing cement. Be sure to leave two or three inches of overlap when you apply the cement.

If you have cut into any of the underlying material and removed it, it will be necessary to build up the hole with more asphalt material or with layers or roofing felt before the surface-level patch is positioned. Coat the patch with roofing cement, allowing two or three inches of overlap. On this area, place an oversized patch of roofing felt, nail it down and coat it with roofing cement. Be sure that there are several inches of overlap in the coating and that all nailheads are completely covered with cement.

HOW TO REPAIR WOOD SHINGLES

Wood shingles are often laid on spaced sheathing, rather than on a solid base. For this reason, take care when walking on a wood shingled roof. It is best to distribute your weight with a ladder hooked to the peak of the roof.

Wood shingles are laid on from the bottom up, in over-lapping courses with alternating edges to prevent rain from finding its way in. Wind-lifted shingles and those which have warped somewhat can be fixed by simply nailing the lifted portions down. However, be sure to drill a nail hole in the shingle to avoid splitting it. And, apply a generous dab of roofing cement over the exposed nailhead to complete the job.

When you've got a leak and you have located it, a fast and effective repair can be made by simply sliding a piece of sheet metal, such as copper flashing, up under the hole. Be sure that the upper edge of the sheet metal slides beyond the hole.

Cracked wood shingles can be cemented together with roofing cement or by applying caulking material. However, be sure to nail down each side of the split and apply roofing cement over the nailheads. Before you split the shingles further, drill the nail holes. Usually one nail in each side of the split shingle, placed at the lower edge, will do the job.

HOW TO REPLACE A WOOD SHINGLE

Wood shingles that never get a chance to dry will rot. Also, falling branches can destroy perfectly good shingles. Whatever the cause, when it becomes necessary to replace a wood shingle, the job must be done carefully. Be especially careful not to damage the underlayer when removing the damaged shingle and replacing it with a new one.

Begin by pulling out all loose shingle material that you can. When you reach a point where portions of shingle cannot be budged, you will have to work a hack saw blade up under the shingle to cut off the nail. Cut these nails off flush with the sheathing.

Now you are ready to measure the empty space to fit a new shingle. Most wood shingles are cut in 16-, 18- and 24-inch lengths; make sure that you have material that is the correct length before you make the replacement. When you have measured and cut the shingle to size, fit it carefully. Be careful not to damage the underlayer as you slide the shingle in place. The shingle should be snug, but not too tight a fit. To help in the final positioning, place a short board at the bottom (wide section) of the shingle and use a hammer lightly on the board to tap the replacement shingle in place. If the board is wider than the replacement shingle, it will stop at the surrounding shingles when you have a perfect alignment.

Nail the shingle in place along the bottom of the shingle above the replacement. Drill pilot holes to prevent splitting the upper shingle and cover the nailheads with roofing cement.

HOW TO REPAIR CERAMIC TILE ROOFS

Ceramic tile roofs are popular on the west coast, and the curved tile version of the material is often referred to as Mission Tile. As a rule, both curved and flat tiles are laid on roofs with very gentle slopes.

Generally speaking, leaks in roofs covered with ceramic

tiles are caused by a misalignment of the tiles. Curved tiles, when used on a gently sloping roof, are often held in place only by their own weight. When there is a steeper slope, the tiles can be wired in place or held with roofing nails. The nails are driven through pre-drilled holes. Of course, broken tiles will almost always produce leaks.

Curved ceramic tile is laid on a roof in alternating convex and concave strips. A series of wood strips is first nailed to the roof, just wide enough apart to accommodate a tile when laid with the concave side facing outward. These base rows are nailed to the sheathing through the pre-drilled holes. Next, the tiles are positioned so that the convex side is facing outward, and each edge fits into adjacent concave tiles. The

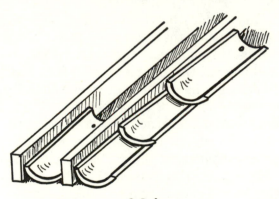

2-9-A
The base tiles are nailed to the roof through
pre-drilled holes.

tiles are laid on in an overlapping fashion, from the botton to the top. When required, they will be nailed to the wood strip that separates the base rows. The cap row, as the exposed course of tile is called, takes the weather. Obviously, water will run between the cap row, but it will be collected and allowed to run down to the gutter by the trough formed by the base row. A tile roof is a very practical roof, and one which should last a long time.

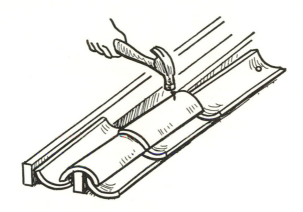

2-9-B
The cap row tiles are nailed and overlapped as shown.

There are two types of tile material—soft-and hard-burned. The hard-burned tile will take the weather much better and it should be used as a replacement, regardless of what type of tile was used on the original roof. If the tiles are not marked to tell you which type they are, lightly strike them with a metal object. A hard-burned tile will give a definite ring, and a soft-burned tile will produce a thunk.

Replacement of curved tile is a simple matter of removing the damaged tile and reinstalling a new tile in its place. But, when this is done, make a careful inspection of the underlayer and repair any tears with fresh roofing cement before installing the new tile.

Flat tiles are made with a shoulder along the upper edge which is hooked over a piece of 1″ × 3″ wood strip nailed to the sheathing. Replacement is a simple matter of lifting out the damaged tile and replacing it with a new tile. Be sure to check the underlayer for rips or holes before positioning the new tile.

The ridge tiles of both varieties are held in position with mortar. When a ridge tile must be replaced, chip away all of the mortar before positioning the new tile. A satisfactory mortar can be made for tile replacement by mixing one part

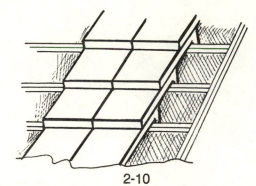

2-10
Flat tiles are hooked over wood roofing strips.

cement, one part lime and six parts of sand. Add enough water as the mixture is made so that it will slide from a trowel, but will still keep its shape when piled on a trowel. Only mix enough mortar for one hour's work. If the repair is not extensive, it is best to buy a ready-mixed bag of mortar, rather than to buy and mix the various ingredients.

HOW TO REPAIR FLASHING

When one section of a roof meets another, or the roof meets a chimney or a vent pipe, flashing is used to seal the joints. The most common flashing material is sheet copper or aluminum, but it is also made of plastic, galvanized steel, lead or aluminum. The repairs described in this section include all points where flashing is used, except at the point where the roof meets the chimney. (See Chapter 4 for details on chimney flashing repairs.)

Most of the metal flashing materials weather well and seldom corrode or develop leaks of themselves. However, flashing joints are sealed with roofing cement, and this material dries out and is a major source of leaks at roofing joints.

As weather changes, wood and other building materials expand and contract. This movement will tug at the joint, and when it is dry and brittle, it will crack. Here's where to look for leaks.

Vent pipes that pass through a roof are mounted in protective skirts and sealed with soft lead necks. If there is a leak at this joint, just use a screwdriver and a hammer to lightly tap the lead against the body of the pipe. It is easy to fix this kind of a leak by applying a bead of aluminized caulking material around the entire joint.

If the leak is found to be at the joint of the flashing skirt and the roof, apply a coating of asphalt roof cement around all of the flashing. Be sure to work the cement up under the shingles above the vent pipe. Be careful when you lift the shingles to expose the flashing. If it is cold, the shingles will be brittle and they can break. Even in warm weather, asphalt shingles will not take a lot of flexing.

HOW TO REPLACE FLASHING ON A VENT PIPE

When it becomes necessary to remove and replace the flashing around a vent pipe, you will have to remove the shingles all around the pipe. See the description of shingle replacement in this chapter for the details of this operation.

Once the shingles have been removed at least six inches all around the stack, place the new flashing over the pipe and

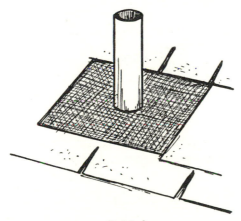

2-11-A
Remove the shingles that surround the vent pipe.

2-11-B
Mount the flashing over the pipe, and nail it down.
Apply a coating of roofing cement over the nailheads
and at the pipe base.

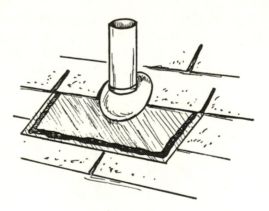

2-11-C
Replace the shingles. If the nailheads show, apply roofing
cement as a protection.

position it on the roof. This should be nailed down on all sides.
Apply a liberal coating of roof cement on the nailheads as well
as around the base of the pipe.

Cover the new flashing with new shingles. It will be necessary to cut the shingle material to fit the contour of the chimney. A pair of tin snips will do nicely when you are working with asphalt material. A coping saw can be used to make the notch in a wood shingle. To make sure that you cut the right size hole, trace the perimeter of the skirt of the flashing and transfer the outline to the shingle before you make the notch.

Nail the shingle down and be sure to cover any exposed nailheads with roofing cement. See the sections on shingle replacement in this chapter for specific information on this repair.

HOW TO REPAIR OPEN AND CLOSED VALLEY FLASHING

When two sections of roof join to form a valley, flashing is laid in the valley before the shingles are applied. This is done to assure that water will not find its way beneath the shingles and into the joint.

The shingles can be applied so that they run to within a few inches of the point where the roofs meet, exposing the underlying flashing. This is known as the open valley method, and it is the most practical way to apply a roof.

When the shingles are applied so that they meet at the valley, completely hiding the flashing, the method is known as closed valley.

The open valley system is easier to install, and it provides less access for water seepage. The only advantage to the closed valley system is that it gives the roof a better appearance.

When the sheets of flashing are installed prior to the roofing, they are laid to overlap about 5", and they are formed to fit the "V" and nailed from the bottom up.

Small, visible holes can be patched easily by using a patch made of the same material used in the original flashing. Apply a coating of roofing cement around the hole and apply the flashing patch. Press the patch in place and then cover the patch and an area of about one inch around it with roofing cement.

Larger leaks usually require that the damaged piece of flashing be replaced. This means that the surrounding shingles must be lifted or removed. Follow the procedures for this job given earlier in this chapter. When the replacement flashing is installed, be sure that it overlaps the sheet below and is overlapped by the sheet above. Replace the shingles on either side of the flashing. If these shingles must be nailed down, cover the nailheads with a dab of roofing cement.

Leaks in closed valley flashing are difficult to locate and tricky to patch. Try to locate the source of the leak from inside the roof before you attempt to lift any of the shingles over the flashing. Once the leak has been located, try to patch the flashing as described above rather than to replace it. If replacement is necessary, remove the surrounding shingles and position a new sheet of flashing. Replace the shingles, and cover all nailheads with roofing cement.

Often it is possible to stop a leak in closed valley flashing by simply pushing a new piece of flashing up under the shingle that covers the leaking flashing. If you run into resistance from a shingle nail, use a hacksaw blade to cut through it to get to the flashing in place.

Would you believe that a dollar's worth of flashing saved a stamp collection worth many thousands of dollars? A routine inspection of a roof once showed that some flashing in a closed valley had worked loose during a storm. The area around the loose copper was soaked, and the owner thought it would be a good idea to check under the roof inside the attic. When he did, he found that months of rain had brought enough water into the attic and onto some plasterboard in the ceiling of a closet so that, at any moment, water could have been dumped onto a valuable stamp collection stored in the closet. By pushing a new piece of flashing up under the shingle, the problem was solved and the stamp collection was saved.

OTHER FLASHING PROBLEMS

Flashing is used to seal many other exterior joints. Where windows join walls and roofs join dormers there is often the possibility of a leak. When such flashing develops leaks, essentially the same procedures are used to effect the repairs that have just been described. Always remember that flashing is applied to prevent water from working back from other roofing material. Whenever you replace flashing at any place on the house, it is important that it should extend beyond the points where water might enter. Wind-driven rain can force water back up under a shingle, and if the flashing is not positioned far enough, the water will flow over it and possibly enter the house.

HOW TO FIX A LEAK AROUND A SKYLIGHT

Once popular a number of years ago, the skylight is now enjoying a new popularity. Some skylights are crude affairs, simply framed into a roof and others are well-designed commercial units, made to fit snugly against rainwater.

Most commercially made skylights are built with their own integral flashing, and they are virtually leakproof. But, if a leak does develop, it can usually be repaired with an application of aluminized caulking compound. Larger holes should be sealed with the application of a patch made of the same material as the flashing. Apply a coating of roofing cement over the hole and position the patch. Cover the patch with the cement and be sure to overlap the patch to seal the edges.

Other skylights are flashed in the same manner as a chimney. If you have any trouble with this type of installation, see Chapter 4. The instructions given for the repair and replacement of chimney flashing are applicable to this problem.

SOME COMMON ROOF-PATCHING MATERIALS

There are several compounds that are used to make roofing repairs, and each has specific advantages. Select the right material for the job and you will prevent problems.

Aluminized caulking material. This compound is mainly used for work on sheet metals. It has a grey color and can be used to patch a rather large hole. It is also ideal for joining two pieces of metal together. If you are inclined to climb a roof in a rainstorm, aluminized sealer can be used on wet surfaces.

Asphalt cement. Asphalt cement is commonly made from plastic and often labeled as plastic asphalt cement. It is thick enough to work with a putty knife, but it can be applied with a stiff brush. It will adhere to metal, wood, asphalt and plastic. Use it directly to seal cracks and small holes, to glue down shingles, seal the edges of flashing and to coat exposed roofing nailheads.

Butyl caulking compound. This material is available in applicator tubes or in bulk cans. It remains pliable after applied, making it ideal for use where flexing is likely to take place. Joints between walls and a chimney will have different temperatures and will expand and contract. An application of butyl caulking to such a joint will stay sealed for a long time.

HOW TO
REPAIR GUTTERS
AND
DOWNSPOUTS

Gutters on a roof do more than prevent you from being drenched when you enter or leave a house in a rainstorm; they collect rainwater and lead it safely away from the foundation. Perhaps the most common cause of a wet basement is either the absence or failure of the system of gutters, downspouts and leaders, and many of the repairs described in this chapter will have the added benefit of solving a wet basement problem.

It's not uncommon for so-called professionals to charge many thousands of dollars to waterproof a basement without first checking for the source of the water. It's true that many damp and leaky basements do require extensive and expensive work to make them dry, but just as many can be fixed permanently without spending a penny. One person I was told of spent over $2000 to do the job only to find that his neighbor, only 20 feet away, solved the same problem simply by adding an extension to his downspout to carry rainwater away from the foundation.

A number of materials are used in the manufacture of rain gutters, and each has its advantages and disadvantages. Regardless of the material, all gutters need regular maintenance, and any problems that occur should be tended to quickly. Perhaps the most obvious problem is a clogged downspout. This can be determined when rain pours over the edge of the gutter, rather than down and out the spout. When this occurs, a number of serious problems can appear. If the back of the gutter is lower than the front edge, water will run over onto the outside wall. Any cracks and holes in the wall will catch the water and lead it quickly inside the house. Even if the water does not show up on an inside wall, it can still cause rot within the wall.

If a gutter is clogged with water before a freeze, the ice that forms can damage or ruin the gutter in short order. Always check your gutters after all the leaves have fallen in the fall and before the freezing weather sets in.

HOW TO CLEAN GUTTERS AND DOWNSPOUTS

Depending on where you live, gutters should be inspected and cleaned at least twice a year. If you live in an area where there are a number of trees, check the gutters even more frequently. Leaves, seeds, pods and other debris can accumulate quickly and clog a gutter before you know it.

It's best to clean your gutters from a ladder, not from a seated position on the roof. Place the ladder so that you are at about waist or chest level with the gutter, and work your way from one end to another. Watch it—don't try to reach too far from the top of the ladder. It doesn't take much of a weight shift at the top of a long ladder before it will topple. It's best to move the ladder two or three feet at a time and do the job in safety.

If your gutter has a painted or a baked enamel surface, be careful that you don't scratch or crack the finish when using cleaning tools. A small hand spade or a stiff brush, such as a whisk broom, can make the job much easier. A hand cultivator can be helpful when the gutter is packed with twigs and small branches.

A downspout will clog if little attention has been paid to the gutter. Leaves, twigs and other debris will catch and ultimately form a tight block. When this occurs, it is often easier to remove the downspout and clean it on the ground than it is to clean it while it is still in place.

Use whatever long prodding tool you can find to do the

job. A rake handle, a dowel, and even a plumber's snake can be pressed into service. But, whatever you use, be careful that you don't puncture the walls of the spout if it is made of thin metal or plastic.

Once the obstruction has been cleared, it is a good idea to run a garden hose part way up the downspout and turn it on full blast for a few seconds. The water will spurt out above you where the gutter is connected to the downspout, so be prepared to dodge a shower. If you want to avoid a drenching, take the hose up the ladder with you and rinse the pipe from the top.

While you are washing the inside of the gutter, have someone check for leaks. All joints should be checked as well as areas where the downspout can be bumped and possibly punctured. If you find any leaks, see the later sections where repairs are described for each of the materials that are used to make the gutters and downspouts.

HOW TO INSTALL LEAF GUARDS AND STRAINERS

The problem of accumulated leaves can be greatly reduced by installing leaf guards over the open portions of your gutters. If you like, you can make the guards from hardware

3-1
Leaf guards can be installed to prevent leaves and twigs
from clogging the gutters.

cloth (coarse wire screen) or you can buy ready-made guards that clip in place easily. If you decide to make your own, get enough ¼″ square mesh so you can cut strips to cover all of your gutters. Use tin snips to do the cutting. These strips can be slipped up under the edge course of shingles on the roof and tacked in place. Don't tack them in place through the shingles; lift them and nail them to the roofing material below. The outer edge of the guard should extend a little beyond the gutter so it can be bent down over the edge.

The ready-made leaf guards are supplied ready for installation, with clips to hold them in place.

These guards keep the leaves, twigs and seed pods out of the gutter, but, after a while, decayed leaves and other particles smaller than the ¼″ squares will fall into the gutter. It will take quite a while, but it is possible for this junk to accumulate to the point where the gutter will be clogged. So, even though you have leaf guards installed, it is important to make periodic checks. The gutters will not become clogged quite as rapidly, but you can still have other problems that must be detected early. If, for example, you have wood gutters, you will want to check them at least twice a year to make sure that no rot has taken place. And, it is a good idea to check metal gutters that can rust to see if this has become a problem.

If you are not especially troubled with a lot of leaves and twigs, you might consider installing leaf strainers rather than going to all of the effort of mounting leaf guards over the gutters. Leaf strainers are little cage-like devices which are inserted in the downspout where it connects with the gutter. They are tapered like plugs and are easily installed; it is just a matter of pushing them into place. These leaf strainers will prevent any accumulation of debris from getting into and clogging the downspout, but, after a while, the junk in the gutter will pile up and prevent any water from flowing into the downspout. If you check your gutters twice a year and are not bothered by a heavy leaf fall, the strainer can be very effective.

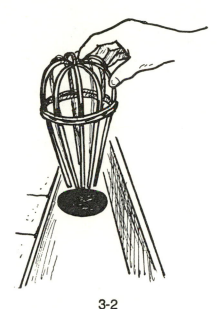

3-2
Leaf strainers, installed at the drain, prevent leaves from
clogging the downspouts.

HOW TO FIX A SAGGING GUTTER

The most persistent cause of a sagging gutter is probably a clog just before a freeze. Water accumulates and freezes; additional snow or rain adds to the problem and the weight pulls the gutter down. Or, the sheer weight of a gutter can cause it to sag over a period of years.

Don't think that because a gutter appears to be straight when viewed from the ground, it hasn't sagged. You will be looking up at an angle, and from this point of view it is difficult to determine if the proper pitch is being maintained.

A gutter should drop about an eighth of an inch for each foot of length as it runs toward the downspout. Anything less than this may make it incapable of handling a large volume of water efficiently. If its pitch is any steeper than this, a heavy rain may cause an overflow at the end.

If the gutter is longer than 35 feet or so, it was probably installed with two downspouts—one at each end. This, of course, means that the gutter must pitch from the middle toward each downspout at the same rate—an eighth of an inch per running foot. Gutters of less than 35 feet are most often installed with one downspout. The pitch is all in one direction—toward the downspout.

If you are unable to determine whether the pitch of your gutter is sufficient to carry off the rain, dump a pail of water in the gutter at the highest point away from the downspout. If your gutter has a downspout at each end, pour the water in the middle. Watch the water run; it should flow steadily, not rush, to the downspout. If there are any puddles left, you will have to correct the pitch.

Correcting the pitch of a wooden gutter, if it is not badly out of alignment, usually involves just pushing the gutter up at the point where the water collects and driving in the nails that are already holding the gutter. If these nails no longer hold, pull them out and re-nail the gutter an inch or two away from the original nail hole. Be sure to fill the old nail holes with putty and paint over them.

Metal and plastic gutters each have hangers which are made especially for the particular system. Gutters mounted with hanging straps can be adjusted by bending the straps slightly, but it is often necessary to remove the hanger and reposition it so that the pitch is maintained. If you remove

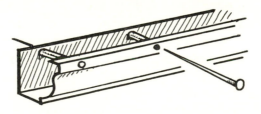

3-3
The sleeve and spike system is one of the more popular
ways of hanging gutters.

and re-nail a hanger, be sure to fill the old nail holes with putty and give them a coat of paint.

Aluminum gutters are often mounted with a spike and tube arrangement. The spike is fitted through the outer edge of the gutter, through the tube, then through the mounting side of the gutter and then driven into the facia board. When these gutters sag, it is usually possible to push up a little at the point where the sag occurs to reposition the gutter. If the sag is too great, or if the nail hole no longer holds the nail and the gutter, it may be necessary to remove the gutter and reposition it completely. However, before this is done, try making a short sheet metal strap and attaching it to the outer edge of the gutter with sheet metal screws. The other end is placed beneath the edge course of shingles and nailed in place with a roofing nail. Make sure that the strap has proper tension so that it takes up the sag.

Metal gutters are assembled in sections, including the corner sections which continue the gutter to the other side of the house. When sags occur, the joints can open up a leak. After the sag has been repaired, be sure to check the joints for leaks; it may be necessary to patch the joints with an application of roofing cement.

HOW TO PATCH A SMALL HOLE IN A METAL GUTTER

If you believe that a hole made by a falling branch in an aluminum gutter can't be repaired, you might end up spending several hundred dollars to have the gutter replaced by a less-than-honest repairman. This happens to many people every day. But if you fix it yourself, and it's a very easy repair, your aluminum gutters just may outlive anything else in your house.

Whether the gutter is made of aluminum, steel or copper, the patching procedure is the same. However, it is important to note that when metal patches are used, they should be made of the same metal as the gutter itself. When two different metals touch each other, a corrosive electrolytic action will take place and cause even more trouble.

If the hole you are going to fix is no larger than the diameter of a quarter, this procedure is best. Begin by using a stiff wire brush to clear away the debris and rust around the hole. Bear down on the brush to brighten and rough up the surface of the metal around the hole.

Next, use a rag soaked in paint thinner to wipe the area clean around the hole, and then apply a generous coating of asphalt roofing cement for a few inches all around the hole.

A piece of heavy canvas or a thin sheet of the same metal as is used in the gutter is then placed over the hole and pressed firmly into the asphalt cement. The cement under the patch should ooze out around the patch.

When the patch is firmly positioned, apply another coat of cement, this time over the patch. Overlap the patch and work it into the joint formed by the edge of the patching material. When the cement dries, you will have a waterproof patch.

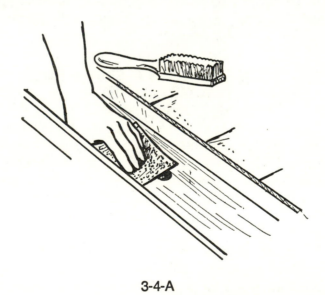

3-4-A

Sweep all the debris from the gutter and then use sandpaper
to roughen the surface to be patched.

3-4-B
Apply a coating of asphalt roofing cement.

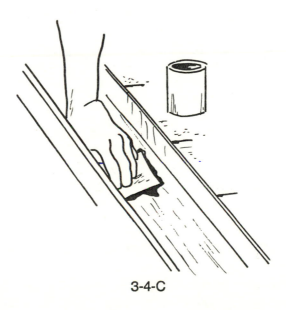

3-4-C

Position a patch of metal or heavy canvas. Apply a coat of
roofing cement over the patch. Overlap the edges.

It's a good idea to paint the underside of the patch that shows through on the outside of the gutter. Use the same paint that was used on the gutter originally. If you don't know the finish, any good paint designed to bond with metal that matches the shade of the original color can be used.

HOW TO PATCH A LARGE HOLE IN A METAL GUTTER

The process of patching a large hole in a metal gutter is essentially the same as patching a small hole, except that a special patch should be made. If the hole is too large, heavy canvas may not be the best material; use the same metal as was used to manufacture the gutter.

In most cases, it is sufficient just to cut a large patch that overlaps the hole by a least an inch, but if the hole is quite large, as might have been caused by a falling branch, you might want to form a patch to suit the contours of the gutter.

Rather than work directly with the metal, make a pattern of stiff paper or light cardboard. Place the edge of the cardboard against the back edge of the inside of the gutter and shape it to match the internal contours. At each place where these are bent, draw it in with a soft pencil. When you have the template, it is a simple matter to transfer the sketch to metal and form the patch without the bother of cutting and trying it on the roof.

Once the patch has been shaped, follow the same patching procedures described in the previous repair. Be sure to paint the bottom side of the patch—that part which can be seen from the ground. Not only will it hide the patch from view, it will prevent any corrosion of the exposed metal.

HOW TO PRESERVE WOOD GUTTERS

Very few wood gutters are installed these days, but if you have them on an old house, or have included them in a new house to harmonize with the style, there are a few things to do to make sure that they last a long time.

If your gutter is painted on the outside but not painted on the inside, the chances are that linseed oil has been used to protect the trough. If this is the case, and the wood appears to be absorbing water, another linseed oil coating is in order. Wait until the gutter is thoroughly dry and brush in a coat. The oil will penetrate the wood, keep it alive and prevent water from doing damage.

If your gutter trough has been painted, you should renew the surface every three years. Make sure that all the loose paint has been scraped off and all debris removed from the area to be painted. After a week of dry weather, you can brush in a coating of paint thinner which is followed by a coat of thinned asphalt roof paint. Give this coat a few days to dry and then apply a second coat. Thinning is important; you want the paint to be drawn into the wood grain. A thick coat will simply lie on the surface and peel off to leave the wood underneath unprotected.

Don't forget the outside of the gutter—but don't use the asphalt paint on it that you used on the trough. Use whatever exterior trim paint that you have used for the rest of the house. For maximum protection and durability, use two light coats.

HOW TO CARE FOR STEEL GUTTERS

Steel gutters are relatively inexpensive, but seldom last as long as gutters made of other materials. You can buy galvanized steel gutters, or you can get them with a pre-applied enamel finish. The enameled steel gutters will last longer then the galvanized types, but any nicks and scratches will open the way for rust.

If you have unfinished galvanized gutters and downspouts, it's best not to paint them until they have weathered for about a year. Paint should be preceded by a coat of special primer. Ask your paint dealer for the brand that he would recommend. There are a number of primers and metal paints on the market and they all work well.

Holes, large and small, should be patched as described in the section on patching metal gutters.

HOW TO CARE FOR COPPER GUTTERS

Copper gutters are quite expensive; the cost of copper is high and the installation is done by soldering all the joints. However, copper is probably the best material that can be used to route water from a roof.

Copper doesn't rust; it oxidizes. This can be seen in the soft green color of the surface. Most people don't paint copper gutters, but the job can be done if the patina of the green copper doesn't harmonize with the color scheme of the house.

If you want to protect the inside of your copper gutters from oxidation, a simple coat or two of spar varnish will do the job. The varnish will not have to be replaced for at least three years. It is also possible to use a light application of roof coating in the copper gutter trough.

Leaks in copper gutters are most likely to occur at the soldered joints. Because the soldered joints are usually small, the leaks will also be small and they can be repaired with a dab or two of roofing cement.

HOW TO CARE FOR ALUMINUM GUTTERS

Aluminum gutters are lighter than those made of wood, steel or copper. They are also easier to handle and to install. And, they offer superior corrosion resistance. All in all, aluminum gutters are probably the best to use in most circumstances. A word of warning, though; they are easily dented and will not take a heavy load for very long. This can be a problem if you have clogged downspouts in icy weather.

Aluminum gutters are supplied either unfinished or with

a factory-applied coat of enamel. If you plan to paint your unpainted gutters, a prime coat is required if latex is to be used. However, special aluminum paints can be applied directly to a well-cleaned surface.

HOW TO CARE FOR PLASTIC GUTTERS

Some plastic gutters are installed with metal hangers in the same fashion as aluminum gutters, and another variety is made with a continuous flange that is nailed to the roof beneath the edge course of shingles. When they are being installed, some room for expansion should be left or there will be buckling. Apart from regular cleaning, there is little you will have to do to plastic gutters; they are virtually maintenance-free. If a falling branch punctures a plastic gutter, you can patch the hole with a conventional plastic repair kit. Leaks at the joints are easily sealed with the mastic that is used to make the joints watertight during installation.

Plastic gutters will not take a heavy load; make sure that no ice forms or that the downspouts do not clog, allowing the gutter to fill with water.

HOW TO INSTALL ALUMINUM GUTTERS

More do-it-yourself gutter installations are done with aluminum than with any of the other materials.

Before you buy any material, make an exact plan of the areas of your house that will be served by the new gutters. Most gutters are made in 10-foot sections, but they are easy to cut with a fine-tooth hacksaw. Every time you connect one section to another or to a corner fixture, or outlet, you will need a slipjoint connector. Be sure to position a downspout every 35 feet, regardless of what was done before. For this installation, you will be using the spike and tube method of hanging. Figure on spiking the gutter every three feet. You will need drop outlets and offset elbows to bring the water to

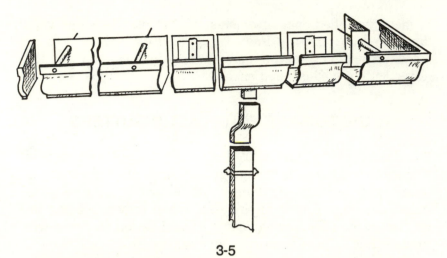

3-5
The basic construction of an aluminum gutter and downspout.

the downspout which should be mounted flush with the side of the house. And, to hold the downspout, you will need wraparound brackets at the top and bottom of the installation. At the bottom of the downspout you will need another elbow plus a leader to carry the water away from the house if the spout is not to be connected to drain tile.

Once you have determined what will be needed and you have bought it, you are ready for the job of installation. Make sure that your ladder is firmly placed because you will be doing a lot of moving about during the process.

Assemble the 10-foot sections to match the length of facia that will support the gutter. To accommodate anything less than 10-foot intervals, the aluminum gutter can be cut easily with an ordinary hacksaw. Be sure to file away any burrs when you cut aluminum; it will make it easier to assemble the sections with the slipjoints. Drill holes through the front and back of the gutter every three feet near the top edge to accommodate the mounting spikes.

Before connecting sections of gutter, apply a bead of caulking to both sides of the slipjoints. Position each side of the two gutter sections within the slipjoint and bend the edge of the joint down against the gutter with a pair of pliers. Corners and outlets are joined in the same fashion.

The gutters are mounted to the facia board by placing a nail through the hole in the outside of the gutter, through a tube, then through the back of the gutter and driving it into the supporting board.

The endcap is mounted by first applying a bead of caulking compound and then pressing it tightly in place.

Important: Make sure that your installation drops about ⅛ inch for every foot of gutter so the water will run off to the downspout. Also, be sure that the outer edge of the gutter is slightly below the level of the roof. This can be checked by placing a board over the roof and the gutter. Doing this will protect your gutters from damage from sliding snowdrifts.

It's best to assemble your gutter system one section at a time. You can support the sections loosely by lightly driving the mounting spikes until all the joints have been made. If you plan the line of the gutter and pencil it on the facia, the job will be a lot easier than trying to maintain the pitch by eye.

HOW TO INSTALL SPLASHBLOCKS

The job of collecting rain in roof gutters and routing it to a downspout doesn't end at the bottom of the leader. The water must be routed safely away from the house, or it will wash away soil and it can find its way into the basement. If the leader isn't emptying into a tile to take the water to a dry well or to the street, you will have to use one of these methods to carry the water away from the foundation.

The most commonly used device to route water from a downspout is a cement or plastic splashblock. This is a trough-like unit which is placed under the end of the downspout and directed away from the house. Several splashblocks can be placed end to end to form a longer trough, but they should be pitched downward as they lead from the house by about 1″ per foot. This is steeper than the grade of a roof gutter, but remember that the splashblock will be carrying all of the accumulated water that has been collected by the gutters, and during a heavy rain there can be quite a bit of water. A lesser grade might result in an overflow, leaving water near the foundation.

In addition to the use of splashblocks there are several other ways in which water can be led from the house. An effective device you can use is a rubberized fabric sleeve that attaches to the end of the downspout. The sleeve can be rolled up when there is no rain, and the action of the collected water in the downspout automatically unrolls it during a rainstorm. These sleeves are perforated so that the water will be distributed over a large area, rather than be concentrated in one gushing burst at the end.

HOW TO INSTALL A DRY WELL

If you live in an area in which storm sewers have been laid, the best bet to get rid of the water is to run a drain tile from the end of the downspout to the road which is served by the sewer. However, if your town doesn't have such storm sewers, you should think seriously about installing a dry well. If you live in a marshy area where the water table is high, your dry well may not be so dry and you will have to find another way to get rid of the collected rain.

Basically, a dry well is a hole in the ground in which there is a pile of rocks and masonry rubble and which has some means to prevent dirt from filling in the spaces between the rocks. The dry well is connected to the downspouts by a drain tile.

Perhaps the best way to make an effective dry well is to begin with a 55 gallon drum. This can be bought new, but it is often possible to pick up a damaged drum from a factory that either uses them to ship chemicals or as waste disposal containers. No matter if it is dented and has a few holes. You are going to add some holes yourself to make it work.

Begin by digging a hole ten feet or more away from the

foundation, but in line with the end of the bottom of the downspout. The hole should be deep enough so that when the drum is placed in it, the top of the drum will be about 2 feet below the surface when the hole is filled.

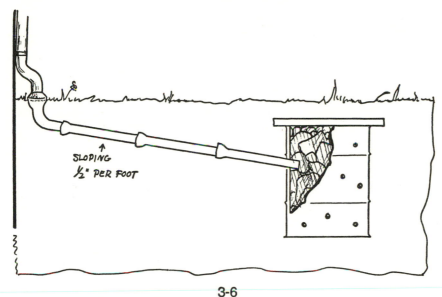

SLOPING ½" PER FOOT

3-6
A dry well, as shown, should not be installed any closer to a foundation than 10 feet.

Next, dig a trench away from the downspout into the hole that will contain the drain tile. The ditch should drop off from the downspout to the point where it enters the hole at no less than ½ inch per foot. Drop the empty drum in the hole temporarily and mark it where the ditch meets its side. Then, pull the drum out of the hole and cut a hole in the side large enough to accommodate the drain tile you are going to use. While you're cutting the hole for the drain tile, punch at least a dozen more holes randomly all over the drum.

When you have the holes punched, put the drum back in the hole and connect the end of the drain tile. The other end of the drain tile should be connected to the end of the downspout. Now, fill the drum with big rocks and whatever broken

masonry material you can find. When it is full, cover the top
with planks that have been treated with a wood preservative
and fill the hole and the trench. The dry well is now ready to
collect all the water that comes its way.

SNOW GUARDS

There are a number of different types of snow guards,
and all are supplied with specific mounting instructions.
Apart from protecting people from an avalanche from the
roof, they can prevent damage to gutters from falling heavy
snow. Generally speaking, the steeper the roof, the more
snow guards that should be installed.

CARING
FOR YOUR
CHIMNEY

Chimneys and the houses they serve live separate but related lives. As the weather changes from hot to cold, the masonry materials used to make a chimney expand and contract at a different rate than the wood of a frame house. As a result, cracks often develop at the joints and water can find its way in easily. When you have water spots on a wall or a ceiling in the area of the chimney, make a thorough check of

4-1
The basic construction of a chimney with two flues. The flue on the left connects with the furnace and the one on the right serves a fireplace.

all the house/chimney joints first, and the chances are good that you will have to look no further.

Before you begin working on your chimney, you should know something of how it is made. The brick chimney you see leading up the side of your house is called a stack and is made of more than brick. The brick actually forms the structural part of the chimney, but the soot and flue gases are conducted upward within the chimney by a column called a flue lining. This lining is a hollow core, and it is assembled in sections as the chimney is built. The liner sections are joined with each other during construction with mortar in much the same way as the bricks are laid.

Before we begin with any of the actual repairs, let's take a look at some ways to protect your chimney.

HOW TO CLEAN A CHIMNEY

Surprising as it may seem, a dirty chimney can be a cause of high fuel bills. When soot collects on the inside of the flue liner, it will slow down the passage of the hot gases. Any change in the balance of the heating system, such as a choked up flue, will adversely affect the efficiency of the furnace. So, it is important that the flue be inspected annually and cleaned when necessary.

Apart from the very real loss of efficiency caused by accumulations of soot, there can be a danger of fire in the chimney. This may seem to be a minor problem; after all, the flue is made of a fireproof refractory material. But, heat from a chimney fire may just be enough to ignite the surrounding structural wood. And, updrafts can carry glowing pieces of soot that can settle on the roof and start a fire. It is obvious that this can be a serious problem, and I urge you to make the inspection discussed in Chapter 1 at least once a year.

If you find a heavy deposit of soot, don't wait too long before cleaning it out. This is a messy job and can be handled efficiently by professionals with their special vacuum cleaners, but it really isn't difficult to do yourself. And, if you're a little careful, it really doesn't have to be a messy job.

Today, more and more people are using wood-burning stoves and attaching them to existing chimneys. Back when an occasional fire was made in a fireplace for decorative purposes, chimneys required very little care. But now there are stories told of those who forgot that wood smoke leaves dangerous deposits in chimney flues. A typical story told of the money saved over other fuels, but then went on to explain how much it cost to rebuild part of the house after a clogged chimney set a fire. The pennies saved in fuel bills hardly made up for the thousands of dollars lost because of a lack of proper chimney maintenance. Most people are cleaning their own chimneys for several reasons. First, there are so few qualified chimney sweeps, and second, when you can find them, they are often quite expensive.

Before you tackle the job, make sure the damper in the fireplace or the door on the ash pit is closed tightly. You will be rustling up a lot of soot in your role as chimney sweep, and, unless you close the damper and ash pit door, you will have a house full of black soot. Believe me, this soot is not like the nice clean ash you can sweep from your fireplace after a winter's eve fire—it's black, oily and darn near impossible to wash from a wall. So, before you do any chimney sweeping, close those doors and dampers.

There are brushes made especially for sweeping chimneys, but if you are unable to find one, you can do a good job with an improvised cleaning device made from an old burlap bag. Fill the bag with straw, wood chips or anything else that will plump it out, yet leave it somewhat pliable. But, before you put in the chips, drop in a few pounds of stones for working weight. Once the bag is filled, tie it closed tightly and attach it to a rope that is a few feet longer than the length of the flue.

Before you clean the chimney flue that serves the furnace, disconnect the duct that connects the flue to the furnace. Seal the flue with heavy paper and masking tape to prevent the loosened material from coming into the house. Also be sure the chimney clean-out door is closed tightly. Now, with everything sealed and the furnace turned OFF, take your rope-and-bag chimney cleaner up to the top of the chimney. Use a flashlight to watch the progress of the cleaning and to see which areas need additional effort.

Begin by lowering the bag into the flue and working it up and down on one side. When you are convinced that the first side is clean, do the same on the remaining sides. You can make the bag big enough to clean all four sides at the same time, but you will have to add quite a bit of weight to make sure it will pull itself down. And, you could run the chance of getting it stuck if there are any obstructions in the flue.

Now that you have scraped all of the sides clean—they won't sparkle—you will have an accumulation of scrapings on top of the damper and behind the furnace chimney clean-out door. Wait a few hours for all the loose particulate matter to settle, then gently open the damper or the clean-out door. Be sure to have newspaper or a big box to catch the soot. When all the loose material has fallen, use a small brush or a stick to poke up around the damper joint to free the soot that has been trapped at the hinge and the joints. If you have cleaned the furnace flue, remove the protective paper and sweep out the soot. Be sure to reconnect the furnace to the flue before you turn it on.

After you have cleaned away the soot, be sure that the ash pit and clean-out doors are tightly closed. As a matter of fact, it is a good idea to seal the door closed with a refractory cement. The next time you want to open the door to clean the pit, the cement can be picked off easily. The reason for this sealing is to insure that there will be no air leaks to reduce the efficiency of the furnace.

As long as you are at it, you should make an inspection of the flue lining for cracks. If you spot any that are within reach, take the time to fill them. Use a stiff mixture of one part masonry cement and three parts sand. Don't forget to wet the area around the crack before applying the patch. If you spot any cracks that cannot be reached easily, have a mason do the job.

You should also check the joint where the furnace and the chimney meet and repair any leaks that you find.

HOW TO INSTALL A SPARK ARRESTER

Technically, this is not a repair, but let's think of it as a way of preventing the need for a major repair—possibly that of completely rebuilding your house. Sparks from wood burning in a fireplace, and incandescent bits of chimney soot in a stack serving an oil furnace, will often blow out the top of a chimney. If they are small enough, they will usually stop burning before they come in contact with anything. But if they are large enough, this "anything" could be your roof, your neighbor's roof, a pile of dry leaves or the top of your brand new convertible. No matter what it is, the chances are very good that there will be a fire.

To reduce this possibility, it is a good idea to add a spark arrester to the top of your chimney. There is no need to buy something elaborate for this; a piece of ordinary hardware cloth cut to fit will do the job nicely. Hardware cloth is not fabric—it's wire mesh. And, it can be cut easily with ordinary tin snips.

Shape the spark arrester as a box to fit over the top of the chimney as shown in the drawing. Do not just fit a piece of mesh over the top and forget it. Anything you put over the top of the chimney, even a piece of wire mesh with big holes,

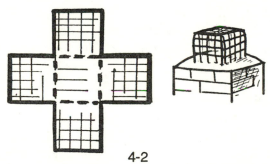

4-2

The pattern for a wire mesh spark arrester. After folding,
the shape can be held by wiring the sides together.

will have some effect on the flow of air and burned gas from the stack. For this reason, make a box as shown and mount it securely above the chimney. To be safe, leave at least six inches between the top of the chimney and the top of the box spark arrester you have made.

You can hold the spark arrester in place by simply wrapping a piece of wire around the unit when it is assembled on the chimney.

Be sure to inspect this arrester periodically. If any leaves, twigs and other material get caught in it, there will be reduced air flow, and it is possible that whatever is caught in it will be ignited by a hot spark. This check can be made from the ground, but it's wise to look closely at the arrester once a year to be sure that any accumulated soot has not closed the holes sufficiently to reduce the draft from the flue.

HOW TO KEEP RAIN OUT OF YOUR CHIMNEY

This, too, is not a repair, but the steps about to be outlined can save you a lot of time and money if you live in an area that has a heavy annual rainfall.

The top of a chimney is open to let out the smoke and waste gases, but it is also open to the rain. Under normal circumstances, rain is seldom a problem in a chimney. However, in areas where heavy rain is common, most masons will automatically build a chimney with a rain cap. This cap is usually a piece of flat masonry, resting on top of four brick pillars at each corner of the chimney. Because this type of cap is usually installed during construction, it's best to use another type of cap if you are trying to solve the problem after the chimney has been made without a cap.

Because it is possible for the inexperienced handyman to make a rain cap that will severely limit the chimney air flow, I suggest that you buy and install a commercial rain cap. The most common type is that which is shaped like a cone and is attached directly to the chimney pot. These caps can also serve as draft deflectors to prevent downdrafts. If you have a fireplace that puts smoke in the room when there is a fair

4-3
A conventional draft deflector.

amount of wind outside, these commercial rain deflectors will probably help solve that problem as well.

Before you trot off to the hardware store to buy your rain cap, you will have to make a trip to the top of the chimney and measure the outside dimensions of the chimney pot. Some flue linings are round—measure the diameter—and others are rectangular—measure the sides.

HOW TO REPAIR FLASHING

Joints made by the meeting of a wall and a chimney, a vent pipe and a roof and different sections of roofing are sealed from the rain with flashing. This flashing can be made of copper, galvanized iron, lead, aluminum, plastic, rubber or tar-impregnated felt. Whatever the material, the job of flashing is to provide a seal against rain at weather-exposed joints.

If the flashing was applied properly, it will seldom cause any problems, but because of changes in temperature and the constant buffeting of wind and rain, some flashing can deteriorate to the point where it begins to admit rain. If you notice water spots in a room and the roof appears sound, check the flashing. Even though the offending flashing may be some distance from the leak, it often turns out to be the location of the problem. Water that leaks through the flashing will often travel along a sloping beam for many feet before it reaches a point where it can invade a room by soaking through a plaster wall or ceiling. So don't rule out flashing as a source of leaks, even though the distance between the flashing and the water spot may be great.

When flashed joints are sealed, the job is usually done with roofing cement. So I suggest that you use this compound to solve your flashing leak problems.

Inspect every inch of flashing on your house; look for holes, big and small. It's surprising how much water can enter through a small hole. Because small holes are less obvious, this job must be done slowly and carefully.

Perhaps the most common source of flashing leaks is the point where the chimney and the house meet. When the flashing has parted from the chimney mortar, it is best to remove enough of the old mortar so that fresh mortar can be used to reseal the flashing. Chip away the dry and crumbling mortar with a chisel, but be careful not to damage the mortar or the bricks in the chimney. After you have cleaned out the dry and crumbling mortar, be sure that the flashing fits back snugly. Then wet the area and refill the joint with patching mortar. This mortar can be a mixture of three parts fine sand and one part cement. Add just enough water to make a stiff but workable mix.

When the mortar is intact, but small openings have appeared in the flashing, you can solve the problem by applying a good coating of roofing cement. While you're at it, this is a good time to coat the entire flashing joint, rather than just the area of the suspected leak. Sometimes leaks aren't too obvious and sealing the entire length of the flashing joint can be the best move.

Where the chimney meets the roof shingles there is also a possibility for leaks. However, it's best to solve this with an application of caulking. For one thing, caulking is not black as is roofing cement, and for another, caulking has sufficient give to expand and contract as the seasons change without opening the joint to the weather. The newer plastic base caulking compounds are especially noted for their flexibility, and are less likely to dry out than the older types.

HOW TO REPLACE FLASHING ON A CHIMNEY

If the flashing has deteriorated enough so that it looks as though patching will only be a temporary measure and one that will have to be repeated regularly, it's best to remove the old material and replace it with new.

Before you start to remove the old flashing, remove the shingles that surround the chimney. Do this very carefully

4-4-A
Remove the caulking that holds the old flashing in place.

with a prying bar, and do not damage the shingles. If you lift each shingle carefully and then pry out the roofing nails, you should have very little trouble. It's best to lift asphalt shingles in the warm weather. When these shingles are cold, they become brittle and can be broken easily. If you can't pry the roofing nails up, use a hacksaw blade under the shingle to cut through the nail.

Next, use a hammer and a chisel to remove the old mortar that has held the flashing which is being replaced. Be careful not to damage the bricks as you work.

4-4-B
Remove the shingles that surround the chimney. Be careful
not to damage them; they will be replaced later.

When the securing mortar has been removed and the shingles taken up, you can start to peel away the old flashing. Do this very carefully because you will be using the old flashing as a template for the new. Also be careful not to damage the roofing paper which lies under the shingles. If you inadvertently do damage this paper, you can patch small holes with an application of roofing cement. A larger hole can be fixed by making a patch of roofing paper and adhering it with roofing cement. After the patch is in place, spread a coat of roofing cement over the entire patch and lap the coat about an inch past the edge.

After all the flashing has been removed, trace it on new copper flashing and cut out the new sections. Fold and make trial fittings before you cement any of the sections in place.

4-4-C
Remove the old base flashing. Do not tear the roofing paper
under the flashing.

4-4-D
Position the new flashing and cement it in place as you go.

When you are sure that each piece will fit perfectly, you can
begin applying the new base flashing with the lowest portion
first. Use roofing cement liberally on the side of the flashing

that will contact the chimney. After the lower section has been applied, put on the side sections, and the top section last.

Once the base sections have been installed, cement the upper, or cap flashing over it. You will have to bend the top of the cap flashing to fit between the bricks in the mortar joints. The cap flashing can be fastened in place either by using fresh mortar or roofing cement. Because the cap flashing will follow the line of the roof, it will have to be stepped upwards at each brick on the sides of the chimney. Be sure to tuck in a folded portion of the flashing all the way up.

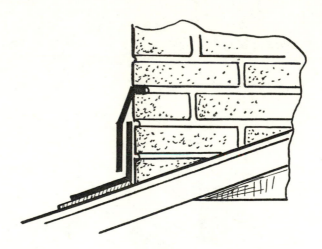

4-4-E
Install the cap flashing over the base flashing. Set the cap into the mortar joints about 2″.

Inspect all your joints, and add cement where necessary.

Once you have the flashing in place and all the seals are tight, you can replace the shingles. Be sure to use large-head galvanized roofing nails. The nails should not be exposed; you will have to lift the upper course of shingles to begin the nailing.

4-4-F
Secure the cap flashing with fresh mortar, or roof cement.

WHAT TO DO ABOUT A LEANING CHIMNEY

There is only one way to handle this problem—call in a professional. Unless you happen to be a mason, this task is really too much for the home handyman. In the first place, the job is very difficult, and in the second, it is very dangerous.

WHAT TO DO IF YOU SEE SMOKE
COMING FROM BETWEEN BRICKS

When smoke makes its way to the outside from between the bricks, it has had to penetrate the flue lining first, and this indicates a dangerous condition. The solution is not just to apply mortar to the brick joint. The main problem lies within the chimney, and a professional should be called in to make an evaluation and to do the repair work.

Smoke issuing from between bricks is a symptom of something much more serious than loose mortar. Don't use the chimney until you have had it checked out.

You may want to check the condition of your chimney to determine if there are any leaks in the flue lining and the bricks and mortar. To do this, build a fire with something that will give off quite a bit of smoke. Damp leaves or straw will do nicely. When it is smoking well, have someone hold a wet cloth over the top of the chimney for a few minutes. Be sure the windows in the room which contains the fireplace are opened. While the cloth is over the chimney pot, examine the chimney carefully for signs of smoke. If you want to do this without having to climb all over the house, use a pair of binoculars or look through the viewfinder of a single lens reflex camera on which you have mounted a telephoto lens. A focal length of 105 to 200 mm is just about right. A longer lens will give you too narrow an angle of vision, and a shorter lens will not give you sufficient magnification.

HOW TO REPLACE CHIMNEY MORTAR

Weather and time take their toll on everything, even something as durable as mortar. When you notice that mortar is missing and that you can pick away pieces quite easily, you should inspect the entire chimney and mark the location of every place where mortar should be replaced. A piece of colored tape can serve as the marker. As you finish each repair, tear away the tape and you'll know how much work you have left.

To do the job, use a chisel to chip away all the loose mortar. Try to get in at least ½ inch, and clean away all loose rubble and dust before you apply the fresh mortar. A word of caution: Chipping masonry can be dangerous. Pieces of loose material will be flying in every direction as you work. Be sure to wear safety glasses before you tackle this job.

Once you have removed all of the crumbling mortar and dusted away the rubble, wet down the area and apply fresh mortar. If you know what mix of mortar was used to make the chimney, prepare the same mix. If you don't know, mix one part masonry cement and three parts of sand. Make a stiff mixture and apply it with a trowel. (See Chapter 9.) You must copy the finishing strokes in the existing mortar, or your work will stand out. Often the tip of the trowel can be used, but when a concave or colonial joint is to be copied, you will have to fashion a pointing tool from a round stick, such as a dowel with the same shape as the existing joint. Be sure to start your pointing while the mortar is still workable. Once it starts to set, it will be difficult, and you will end up weakening the joint with your effort.

If you have a lot of joints to fill, don't wait until you have filled them all before you begin pointing. The mortar may have begun to set by then. Trowel in a few courses, then go back to finish the joint with your pointing tool.

A word of caution: In hot, dry weather the mortar will set a lot faster than it will on a damper, cooler day. Be sure to take this into account when you are working.

As mortar ages, it darkens. Fresh mortar can look mighty stark against a wall of weathered mortar, so try adding mortar color, which you can get at most hardware stores, before you work. Make the mortar just a little darker than the old mortar; it will lighten when it dries.

HOW TO REPLACE LOOSE CHIMNEY BRICKS

If mortar has dried enough, it is possible for bricks to become loose. If the brick is loose enough to remove, just slip it out, but the chances are that it will just wiggle a little, and you're going to have to chisel away the surrounding mortar. Use a small cold chisel, a hammer and be sure to wear your safety glasses. Work at the mortar in small steps to avoid the possibility of damaging the brick. Just keep chipping away until you can pull the brick free.

Once you have the brick in hand, use the chisel to remove any attached mortar. Watch it—you can break the brick quite easily.

Use your hammer and chisel to remove all of the mortar in the hole left by the brick. Before you replace the brick, be sure to clean away all of the dust and rubble from the hole.

Wet the hole, and apply a layer of fresh mortar all around the inside. Use more mortar than you think will fit after the brick has been repositioned—the brick will fit snugly and displace any excess mortar. Wet the brick and press it in place. When it is positioned correctly, re-point the joints and the job is done.

HOW TO REPAIR A CHIMNEY CAP

A chimney is made of a surrounding structure of some masonry material such as fieldstone or brick, and a flue liner which is made of a special refractory material. At the top of the chimney, the joint of these two structures is sealed with mortar and this seal is called a cap. The cap is applied in a slope so that water will run off easily. Because of the exposure to weather, and the constant changes in temperature as the furnace goes on and off, the cap can crack and chip away easily. When this happens, rain can get in between the stack and the liner. If enough rain collects, there can be serious problems. As was mentioned in Chapter 1, the cap should be checked regularly—at least once a year, and more often if possible.

If you discover that the cap has cracked, or that some of the masonry has chipped away, be sure to make the repair right away. Chip away the loose, dry mortar, and dust out the pieces. Wet the surrounding area and apply a patch of fresh mortar. Use one part masonry cement and three parts sand with enough water to make a stiff but workable mix.

If you are restoring a section, rather than just filling in cracks, trowel the mortar on in several layers, and be sure to follow the slope of the original cap. You want to make sure that the rain will run away and not have a chance to collect. Preventing water from collecting is especially important in areas where the winter brings freezing temperatures. When water freezes in masonry cracks, it will expand and cause serious damage.

FIREPLACE PROBLEMS

Technically speaking, the fireplace is not part of the exterior, but it is part and parcel of the chimney, and I think some words of caution are needed. Open joints in a fireplace are a fire hazard. You should inspect the interior of your fireplace regularly and make any repairs that are necessary.

To fill cracks and replace brick inside a fireplace, be sure to buy mortar mix that contains fire clay. Conventional mortar should not be used for the job.

THE CARE
AND REPAIR
OF SIDING

If an exterior wall isn't watertight, you can have all kinds of problems in your house. Yet, this wall, which must keep out the rain, must allow a certain amount of water vapor to pass through it. Wood and masonry materials do permit this exchange of vapor, and it is possible to install vents in the walls to insure that water vapor passes through materials that are either heavily painted, or made of materials which act as a barrier to the vapor.

Most water problems occur at the various construction joints. Where a wall meets a window or a door for example, there is great potential for rain to find its way inside. These joints are best sealed with a caulking compound that remains somewhat flexible to accommodate the expansion and contraction of the materials in the joint as seasonal temperature changes take place. Before any of the repairs are explained, it is important to know something of caulking materials and how to use them.

HOW TO CAULK EXTERIOR JOINTS

Water leaks, heat loss in the winter, cooling loss in the summer, as well as mildew and rot, are all problems you can have if you neglect dried-out caulking in your home.

Don't wait until you spot a damp wall or find water leaking in to check the condition of your caulking. It's just a matter of inspecting the various exterior joints and picking at the caulking material with the blade of a screwdriver. The caulking compound should be resilient, and it should fill the gap completely. Also, be sure that the caulking is adhering to both sides of the joint being sealed. If you find that any of the joints fail the inspection, don't waste a minute—recaulk.

Here are the major places to check on your caulking inspection:

- Where the chimney contacts roof shingles and siding
- Between dormer and roof shingles
- Between window sills and siding
- Between window frames and siding
- Between siding and an entrance overhang
- Between siding and a door frame
- Between masonry steps, porches, patios, and house foundations
- Between the underside of eaves and molding
- Between siding and a deck roof
- At corners formed by siding
- Between siding and vertical corner boards
- Where outside water faucets extend from the house

Caulking can be used in many other places, as well. It is often used to seal small cracks in masonry and brick work. It is also used to seal flashing, and this process is described in Chapter 4.

Of all the places where caulking is used in home construction, there are four points where a good seal is especially critical. It pays to make a yearly inspection of these areas and to replace any dried caulking immediately. These points are:

1. The joint formed by siding and windows and doors should be checked annually. The top of the header is especially susceptible to leakage problems. It's the most inaccessible spot, but it pays to drag out the ladder to check carefully.

2. Look within the frame of your windows and doors

5-1
Caulking should be used to seal the joints formed by a
window frame and siding.

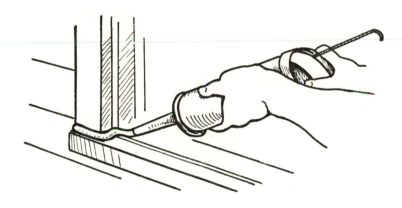

5-2
Seal the joints around the sill with caulking.

very carefully. Water can get in and do extensive
damage here.

3. Where pieces of siding are joined, gaps are formed. The crack between shingles, and the gap that occurs between lengths of clapboard as temperature changes occur are prime spots for leakage.

4. Look at spots where porches, decks and roof additions meet the house. Wherever a flat surface abuts a wall, there is a potential for leakage that can be prevented by the use of caulking.

Is all caulking alike? No, and the number of different types being offered today can lead to confusion. However, if you want to use one material that has the widest application, it should be one of the butyl compounds. This is the caulking that is used most often during construction by builders, and it retains its flexibility longer than some of the other types. This flexibility is very important. As weather changes, construction materials expand and contract. When a gap is sealed with caulking, the material should be elastic enough to give as these changes take place. If the caulking is stiff, it will crack, and you will have leakage problems. Another advantage of the butyl material is that it takes paint very well.

The butyl material is sold in cans for bulk use, in small tubes, and in cartridges for use in a caulking gun. If you have a lot of caulking to do, it's a good idea to invest in a caulking gun. It speeds up the work, and helps to make an excellent seal.

If you are unable to get any of the butyl material, here are the characteristics of other types of caulking to help you make an appropriate selection.

• **Silicone caulking.** This is a very long-lasting caulk, and it adheres well to just about all surfaces, except those that have been painted. If you must use this caulking over paint, rough up the surface on which it will be applied. This will help make a better bond. If you can sand down to the bare wood, you will make an even better bond.

• **Oil base caulking.** Until the development of the various plastics, this was once the most popular caulking compound. It is still used extensively, but it will dry out in time. It will bond well with just about any surface.

- **Latex caulking.** This is a water-based material which dries rapidly, and takes paint very well.
- **Polyvinyl acetate.** This caulking material adheres well to just about all surfaces.

Unlike paint, you can only buy caulking compound in three colors—white, gray and black. But you can tint caulking by adding oil paint pigments and kneading the material until the color matches and is evenly blended. If you are going to tint caulking, start with the white material.

In addition to the containers in which caulking is supplied, it is also sold in a rope-like shape, wound on a spool. To use it, simply unwind the amount needed, and press it into the crack with your fingers or a putty knife.

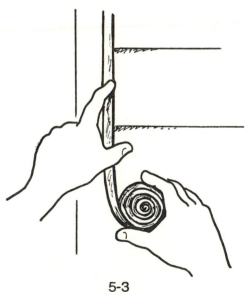

5-3
Caulking is also available in rope form.

HOW TO PREPARE A SURFACE FOR CAULKING

If this is a repair, begin by removing all of the old caulking from the crack. Never apply caulking over existing dry material, except in an emergency. You can remove old, dry caulking with the blade of a screwdriver, but the most convenient tool for the job is a small putty knife or paint scraper. If you can arrange it, wait for the warm weather—the job will go a lot easier.

Before any caulking is applied, regardless of the material selected, be sure that the surface is entirely dry. Wait three or four days after a rain before doing the job.

Once the old caulking has been removed completely, go over the area with a stiff wire brush. This will not only remove the tiny particles that could prevent total adhesion, it will also roughen up the surface to provide a better seal with the new caulking.

After the wire brushing, wipe the surface with a solvent such as turpentine or paint thinner. This will dissolve any residue which may have been left on the surface.

If you are caulking fresh wood, and not using a silicone based caulk, you should paint the surface with a thinned exterior paint or thinned linseed oil. This is especially important if you are using an oil based caulk. If the wood surface is not painted, it will draw oil from the caulk and dry it very quickly. You can also use a thinned, quick-drying varnish as a sealer.

If you are filling a thin crack, don't bother with a cartridge caulking gun—the job is best handled with a small can of caulking compound and a putty knife. Just scoop out a little caulk from the can and press it firmly into the crack in steps until it has been filled. Smooth out the edges and let it dry.

Larger caulking jobs, such as sealing the joints between walls and windows and doors are best handled by using a caulking gun. To load the gun, pull the handle all the way out to make room for the cartridge. Load the cartridge so the tip protrudes from the slot in the front. Use a knife or heavy duty

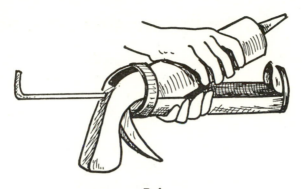

5-4
Pull out the plunger completely before loading a
caulking cartridge.

scissors to nip off the tip, and then punch the seal under the tip. Squeeze the handle until the caulking begins to flow steadily. Squeeze the trigger with only enough pressure to produce a steady flow of caulking as the tip is drawn along the crack. Hold the gun at a 45° angle and make sure a wide bead of the material covers the crack. Move the tip at a slow enough rate to insure that caulking fills the crack, covers both sides and beads up over the crack.

If you have any especially wide cracks to fill, it is a good idea to first pack the hole with oakum. This rope-like material will act as a filler and insulation, and make it easier to do a good caulking job.

You may not pay much attention to the siding of your garage and think that very little can go wrong there. But let me tell you about the problems that one person had. The joint formed by the door frame and the clapboard siding on his house had opened up—just a little. But this opening was enough to let in a little water every time it rained. The water collected around the sill and gradually rotted many feet of wood. The cost to repair this damage compared with the price of a little caulking was staggering. For $2 worth of caulking and a few minutes time, the owner could have saved almost $2000 in professional repair bills.

HOW TO STRENGTHEN WARPED CLAPBOARD

Clapboard is nailed in place, but it can warp if it has not been properly cured, or if it has been exposed to dampness. Whatever the cause, the solution is the same.

Drill pilot holes at the high points of the warp, or as near as possible if you can position the hole over a stud. Then, drive wood screws through the clapboard and into the stud to pull the warp down flat. It may take several screws in different locations, but this remedy will usually solve the problem if the warp is not too severe.

Be sure to countersink the screws and fill over the heads with putty before painting. If you suspect that the warping was caused by internal dampness, you should try to locate the source of the moisture and correct the problem.

HOW TO REPAIR SPLIT CLAPBOARD

Clapboard splits usually run with the grain along the

5-5-A
Apply a coating of waterproof glue to both edges of
split clapboard.

length of the board. Unless you have a big split, the repair can be handled very effectively with some waterproof glue.

Make sure that the board is dry before you make this repair. Begin by prying the lower section of the split board away from the house to expose the edge of the split lower section. Coat the edge with a good waterproof glue, and then reposition the lower section. Before the glue begins to dry, drive a few finishing nails into the board just below the damaged section. The nails should touch the bottom of the damaged section and only be driven in about a half inch. When the nails are in position—about every two inches along the bottom of the cracked section—bend them upwards slightly. This will put enough pressure on the split section to insure that the glued joint will dry firmly.

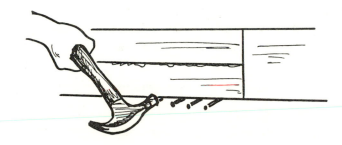

5-5-B
Freshly glued clapboard is clamped temporarily by driving
a few nails lightly into the boards below.

After the glue has dried, remove the nails and putty up the nail holes. Try not to get glue on the outside surface of a piece of clapboard; paint doesn't adhere to most wood glues and, if you plan to paint, you could have problems.

To add strength to a repair, you can drive a few finishing nails in the cracked section at the point where the board meets the next section. Be sure to countersink the nails and fill the heads with putty.

HOW TO REPLACE A SECTION OF CLAPBOARD

When a section of clapboard is too badly damaged to patch, it's best to remove it and replace it with a new section. This may seem difficult, but it's actually rather easy—if you follow these step by step instructions.

Before you remove the old section, make sure that you can get a replacement section of the same style. Often, styles of clapboard are discontinued by mills, and it may be necessary to fashion a replacement from unfinished stock. This can be difficult, but not impossible. However, if you find that one lumber yard no longer carries the same run of board, try all the others in your neighborhood before you give up.

You are going to have to saw out the old section, and a back saw is the most convenient tool for this task. And you are going to have to make sure that the saw cuts are parallel and at perfect right angles to the section above. Mark the saw cut line using a steel square, and position the cuts a few inches past the damaged area into solid wood.

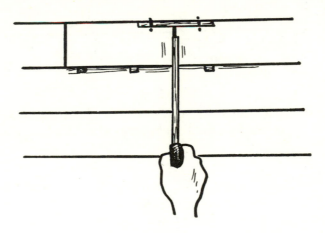

5-6-A
Use a back saw to cut both sides of the section of damaged clapboard. The blocks above and below the board protect other wood during the cutting.

Before you begin cutting, drive a few small wood wedges up under the section to be cut out and hold a piece of scrap wood over the good clapboard under the damaged section where you plan to cut. These two steps will help prevent you from damaging any good board.

Make the saw cut at both ends of the damaged section. The board will still be attached under the course of board above. You can now break out the exposed section of clapboard. It's best not to try to break this off in one large section; you could damage the board above. Use a chisel to split off strips two or three inches wide until you come to the end of the saw cuts.

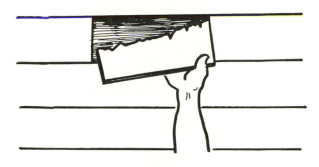

5-6-B
Break out the damaged section of clapboard after it has been sawed through. Use a pry bar or a similar tool to remove the remaining parts of the damaged clapboard.

To remove the piece of board still left under the upper board, you will have to saw through the nails that held it in place. You can use the metal cutting blade on a turret saw, or a hacksaw blade with a makeshift handle made by wrapping one end in an old rag.

After the nails have been sawed through, you can use a pry bar or a chisel to pull free the remaining section.

Before you replace a new section of clapboard, be sure that the building paper under the boards is intact. It is highly likely that it will be somewhat damaged by the process of removing the damaged section. Any tears can be easily patched with asphalt cement. If big sections have been damaged, make a patch of new building paper, and fasten it in place with asphalt cement. Cover the outer edges of the patch with cement, once it has been positioned.

When you are sure that the building paper is intact, you can measure and cut the replacement board. It should be a snug, but not tight fit. To fit the new section, hold a piece of scrap wood at the bottom edge and tap with a hammer until it is in place.

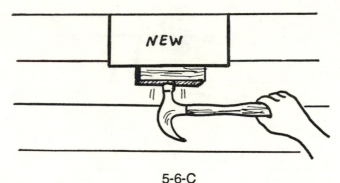

5-6-C
After cutting a new board to fit snugly, drive it in place with a hammer and a piece of protective scrap wood.

Nail the new section in place, using the same nailing pattern that was used in the original construction. Countersink the nails and fill the holes with putty.

Both edges of the board should be caulked before any paint or stain is applied.

HOW TO STRENGTHEN A WARPED WOOD SHINGLE

Warped wood shingles can be flattened by simply nailing the high side of the warp down. Be sure to use either galvanized or aluminum nails, and countersink the heads. Fill the countersunk holes with putty, and repaint.

HOW TO REPLACE A DAMAGED WOOD SHINGLE

Wood shingles, or shakes, should be removed and re-placed if they are badly cracked or damaged. To do this, it is necessary to cut through the nails that hold the shingle in place.

You can use the metal-cutting blade of a turret saw, or it is possible to improvise a saw by wrapping one end of a hack-saw blade with an old rag. Slip the blade up under the lower portion of the shingle above the damaged shingle. Saw through all of the nails. These nails not only hold the lower portion of the shingle above, but they also hold the top of the damaged shingle.

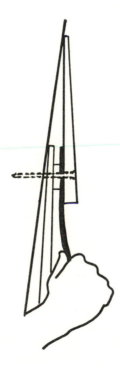

5-7
Use a hacksaw blade to cut through the nails that hold shingles in place.

Next, slip the blade up under the lower edge of the damaged shingle and cut through the nails. Use a hammer and chisel to split the damaged shingle in several parts. Be careful not to cut into any of the building paper under the shingles. However, if you do slip, the cuts can be repaired with asphalt cement.

When the shingle has been split, you will be able to pull it free. Next, use pliers to remove all of the nails that hold the damaged shingle in place. Be careful not to damage any of the surrounding shingles.

Before you slip in the replacement shingle, check the building paper and make any repairs, if necessary.

Trim and fit a replacement shingle. It should fit snugly but it should not be tight. Slip the new shingle in place and nail the top and bottom with aluminum or galvanized nails.

HOW TO REPLACE ASBESTOS SHINGLES

Asbestos shingles are brittle and can be damaged easily. Therefore, care should be taken during repairs not to damage surrounding shingles.

Asbestos shingles are not nailed top and bottom, as are wood shingles. They are held in place by nails near the bottom only. So, when you must remove such a shingle, it will only be necessary to cut through one row of nails. See the instructions for cutting nails in the section on wood shingle repair.

When you lift the damaged shingle, or parts of it, from the wall after cutting through the holding nails, be careful that you don't put much pressure on the lower edge of the shingle above. These shingles have no give at all, and it is easy to damage surrounding siding.

Check the building paper under the damaged shingle and patch any holes or tears with asphalt cement. Next, you can slip the replacement shingle in the opening and nail it in place. Be sure to drive the nails through pre-drilled holes in the same position as the nails in the surrounding siding.

HOW TO MIX STUCCO

Cracks and holes in a stucco wall can be patched with a packaged mortar mix, or you can make your own by blending one part masonry cement and three parts sand. Be sure that the sand is washed clean, or it will not only weaken the patch, it will also discolor it.

Blend the masonry cement and sand first and then add enough water to make a workable but firm mix. You should be able to make a small pile of the material without having it settle.

If you are working with a colored stucco wall, you can add pigments to the mix to match the color. The weight of the added pigment should never exceed 5 percent of the weight of the masonry cement, or the patch will be weakened. To make sure that your blend of color is right, it is usually a good idea to make test mixes first, and let them harden before making the final mix. It is surprising how much a patch will stand out, even when it is only slightly lighter or darker than the surrounding wall.

HOW TO PATCH SMALL CRACKS IN STUCCO

Use a knife, screwdriver blade or the edge of a paint scraper to widen the crack somewhat. This step will trim away any damaged and weakened stucco around the crack.

To make sure that the stucco patch will hold, it is necessary to prepare an undercut. That is, the back of the crack will have to be wider than the exposed part. To do this, use a small chisel and a hammer to cut under each side of the crack. Hold the chisel at a sharp angle and place the blade into the crack. Tap the end of the chisel and move the blade along the length of the crack. Do this to both sides of the crack, but be careful not to damage the edge of the previously undercut side.

When the undercut has been made, brush away all of the

dust and debris very carefully. Then, wet down the crack and the surrounding wall. The area should be damp, but not wet with water.

Use a putty knife, trowel or a paint scraper to pack the hole with freshly-mixed mortar. Pack the material in tightly. If the crack is deep enough to go all the way through the stucco layer, overfill the crack slightly, and wait for about 15 minutes. Then, use your packing tool to work the level down to that of the surrounding wall.

The patch and the surrounding area should be dampened by a fine mist from a garden hose twice a day for two or three days. If the weather is exceptionally hot and dry, you can dampen the area more often.

HOW TO PATCH LARGE HOLES IN STUCCO OVER A WOOD FRAME

Stucco is usually applied to a metal lath on wood framing or on a wall of concrete block. Many of the steps in repairing either construction are the same, but the points can be best illustrated by beginning with patches made.

Begin the job by breaking away all of the loose stucco. When this is done, the chances are good that some of the metal lath will have been damaged, and there may be holes in the undercoating of building paper. Be sure to patch all holes in the building paper with liberal applications of asphalt cement, and re-wire the broken joints in the metal lath. Don't use aluminum wire to patch the lath; aluminum has an adverse reaction to the ingredients of the cement used in the patch.

Three separate patching steps are required to fill a hole properly in a stucco wall. The first and second coats are made of a mixture of one part Portland cement and three parts coarse sand. Mix the dry ingredients first and then add enough water to make a fairly stiff mixture.

The first patch is called a scratch coat, and it is applied to within ¼ inch of the outside edge of the hole. Be sure to force the material in and around the wire lath to insure a strong bond. The edges of the hole should be thoroughly dampened before the patching material is applied. There are plasterer's trowels that make the job easier, but you can use anything from a pointing trowel to a paint scraper. It really doesn't pay to buy special tools if you have only a few patches to make.

As soon as the scratch coat begins to firm up in the hole, but before it actually hardens, you will have to make a series of deep scratches in the surface. You can do this with a nail, or you can make a small rake by driving some nails into a small board.

The scratch coat should be kept dampened for two days. Use a fine spray from a garden hose to do the job. If the weather is exceptionally dry you might have to spray the patch twice a day.

The second, or brown coat, is made of the same mixture as the scratch coat. Trowel on the brown coat to within ⅛ of an inch of the surface of the hole, but smooth it out carefully. Keep the second coat dampened for two days, too.

The third patch—the finish coat—is made of one part Portland cement, three parts sand and one quarter part lime. Mix it with enough water to make a stiff paste. The finish coat is troweled in, and then smoothed evenly with the edges of the hole by raking it over with a straight edge. A sandy finish is accomplished by a final troweling just as the patch begins to set. The textured finish, common to many stucco walls, is made by swirling the surface with a stiff brush. Don't spray the finished patch with water for a day. Then, use a fine spray to keep the patch damp for one day.

HOW TO PATCH A HOLE IN STUCCO OVER A CONCRETE BLOCK WALL

Stucco is also applied over masonry walls, but the metal lath is not used as it is in frame construction. Begin by chipping away all loose stucco and then roughing up the exposed surface of the masonry wall. Use a wire brush to remove all of the debris, and then soak the exposed block and the surrounding stucco.

This type of surface can usually be patched with only two coats—the scratch coat and the finish coat. The same steps should be followed as outlined for the repair of stucco over a wood frame, except that the first coat is applied directly to the block wall, and the brown coat is eliminated.

In some types of construction, stucco walls extend to and beneath the ground. Little cracks in stucco may seem harmless, but consider the plight of one person who found that such a small crack just below the ground level had become the entry for termites. Fortunately for this person, the crack was spotted early and before the termites had a chance to do any serious damage. Once the ground around the foundation had been treated with an anti-termite chemical, the crack was sealed and a major disaster was averted. It was estimated that the termites could have caused over $5000 in damages if the crack had gone undetected for a year. For a total of $20 spent for patching compound and anti-termite chemicals, the owner of this house saved a fortune.

HOW TO REPAIR BRICK WORK

For a complete description of how to handle repairs of brick and masonry walls, see Chapter 9.

HOW TO SOLVE PROBLEMS OF MILDEW

When the weather is warm and damp, and the side of your house that never gets any sunshine begins to have dark blotches, it's probably mildew. Actually, the cause of this problem is a mold, and even if you've never had it before, this doesn't mean that it won't occur under the right conditions.

When mildew appears on an exterior painted surface, it

is usually black, although, depending on the strain, it can be just about any color of the rainbow. It's been known to grow under a freshly painted surface, even on the sunny side of the house. But it is most often noticed in the shade.

To make sure that you have a mildew problem, and not just a dirty wall, you can run two simple tests. First, look at the blotches with a magnifying glass. The color should be uniformly dark, and it should grow in clusters. The color of dirt will be inconsistent, and you should be able to spot some texture, which will be absent if the problem is really mildew.

The best test is done with a little household bleach. Rinse the surface of one of the blotches with bleach and wait for two or three minutes. If you do have mildew, the rinsed area will begin to lighten noticeably. If it's dirt, there should be no color change.

If you do have a mildew problem, you can solve it by washing the surface with this easily made remedy:

> 3 ounces of trisodium phosphate (This can be bought in most hardware stores, but if it is unavailable, use Soilax, Oakite or Spic and Span)
>
> 1 ounce of powdered detergent
>
> 1 quart of household bleach
>
> 3 quarts of warm water

Use a medium hard brush to scrub all of the affected areas. It's best to wash a bit beyond the affected area to insure that the blight will not spread. Scrub well and rinse several times with fresh water. Be sure to wear rubber gloves and safety goggles, and protect shrubbery in the area from splashing solution.

This treatment will kill the mildew that is on the wall, but it won't prevent it from returning, given the same weather conditions. If you are planning to paint the affected area, you can use a mildew-resistant paint, or you can add a commercial mildew preventer to the paint before you begin the job.

Once I heard of a man who decided to paint his house

after getting what he thought were very high estimates from professional painters. He read everything he could about painting, and asked a lot of intelligent questions of the paint store owner. But he made one serious mistake; he assumed that the dark blotches on his north wall were mere patches of dirt.

He washed the wall thoroughly and then proceeded to apply paint in a very professional way. But what he took to be dirt was really mildew, and it soon destroyed his beautiful paint job. It's too bad that he didn't try the tests outlined in this chapter. Be sure that you do, or a lot of effort and money can be lost to mildew.

HOW TO
PAINT AND PRESERVE
EXTERIOR SURFACES

Paint doesn't last forever, and, unless the surface is prepared properly and the right paint is applied in the right way, you can end up doing a paint job every year. It pays to take a little time to diagnose the cause of your painting problem and to prepare the surface properly. Read this list of problems and compare your problem with the illustrations. When you can identify the cause of your surface troubles, you will be a long way toward finding a practical solution.

HOW TO SPOT ALL PAINT PROBLEMS

Blisters: Blisters are bubbles in the paint. If you push them, they will collapse and you will often find them either damp inside, or filled with water. It is the moisture, or water,

6-1
Moisture in the wood causes paint to blister and peel.

that causes a blister. This moisture comes from behind the wall and works its way to the outer painted surface. The problem only occurs with oil paint because this cover doesn't breathe; it doesn't allow moisture to pass through it. Latex paint does allow moisture to pass through it without making blisters. But do not apply a coat of latex paint over a coat of blistered oil paint and hope to solve your problem. It will be necessary to remove all of the oil paint first, and to apply a coat of latex primer before applying the finish coat of latex paint.

The best solution to blistering is to try to eliminate the source of the water or moisture. If the blistering is located in only one area of the house, the job will be a lot easier. For example, you will find that the wall outside a bathroom where many hot showers are taken will be subject to blistering. The warm, moist air from the shower finds its way between the inside and outside walls, and then works its way through to the painted exterior surface. When the moisture is stopped by a barrier of oil paint, it simply lifts the paint to make those ugly blisters.

You may also find an area under a faulty gutter that has blistered. Correcting the pitch of the gutter or cleaning the downspout to prevent an overflow will often correct the problem.

Areas around windows and chimneys can suffer from the problem if the joints are not tightly caulked. Check the caulking and repair leaks before doing any painting.

If you find that the blisters are all over the house, you will know that the moisture is coming from inside and you will either have to do an elaborate insulation job or scrape off all the old oil paint prior to resurfacing with latex. If the blistering is confined to the walls outside the bathroom or kitchen, it is often easier to install a ventilating fan to draw off the warm moist air. Most new houses are built with a continuous vapor barrier or plastic sheet in the walls. This is very effective, but impossible to add to a finished house. If your house is in the making, be sure to include this barrier.

Peeling: When every coat of paint on the house peels, right down to the wood, it is the result of moisture and the blisters described above. The blisters simply get bigger and bigger until they split, leaving the wood exposed.

However, when one coat of paint peels from another, the chances are good that the original surface was not prepared properly. A very glossy first coat will not hold a second coat, and a surface that is greasy will reject another coat of paint. Ordinary grime that settles on the outside walls is often enough to prevent a second coat from sticking. Wash the walls with a good household detergent to get rid of the grime, and sand a glossy surface to make sure that the next coat sticks.

Peeling can also be caused by a delay in the application of a second coat of paint. Most paint manufacturers state that if a second coat is to be applied, it should be put on no later than 14 days after the first coat.

Chalking: Chalking is a normal occurrence in exterior paint. It is the gradual disintegration that takes place as the paint ages. In fact, it can be beneficial, especially in light colored paints. The chalk is actually the gradual breakdown of the surface, and is seen as a white powdery substance on the surface. When this occurs on light paint, any accumulated dirt and grime falls away with the chalking paint.

Chalking also makes future painting a lot easier. The layer of paint that chalked is a lot thinner than it was when it was first applied. If chalking did not take place, the build-up would be soon very difficult to cover.

Paints that chalk should only be used on the siding, not on the trim. And chalking paints should never be used on wood which is above a masonry surface. Chalking paints will leave streaks after rain, and paints used on trim and above masonry can stain siding paint and masonry below the painted wood.

Chalking, when it is excessive, is a serious problem. It can mean a very short life for a paint job.

Excessive chalking is usually the result of a coat of paint

that is applied too thinly. Some paints have better hiding qualities than others and there is often a tendency to try to get away with one coat when it appears to cover very well. However, when this coat is over a porous surface, the binder can be absorbed quickly, leaving only the pigment which chalks rapidly. Two coats are usually better than one, in this case.

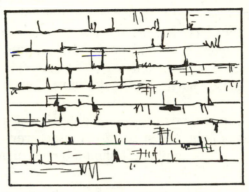

6-2
When a second coat of paint is applied before the first has
dried, the effect is called alligatoring.

Checking and alligatoring: Checking and alligatoring are really the same thing. Checking is the early stage and alligatoring is the most noticeable disfigurement. Think of the skin of an alligator and you will get the idea. A lot of connected cracks that ultimately look like a network of connected boxes characterize the problem of alligatoring.

When the second coat of a two-coat paint job does not contain sufficient binder, you will get checking and alligatoring. The remedy is to use the best paint you can buy.

The problem can also be caused by an overanxious painter. Applying a second coat over a prime coat that has not been given enough time to dry will produce the same result.

The only remedy is to scrape away the offending paint, sand the surface, and repaint.

Cracking and scaling: Checking and scaling affect only the top coat of paint, but cracking goes right down to the bare wood. This problem is usually the result of a paint that is not flexible enough to expand and contract with the wood surface as the weather changes. As cracks appear, they allow water and moisture to get behind the paint to speed up the process of peeling.

To solve this problem, the offending paint must be scraped off and a coat of more flexible paint should be applied.

A different type of cracking takes place when too many layers of paint have been allowed to build up. Usually referred to as cross-grain cracking, this problem can be spotted by the cracks that appear across the grain of the wood. To solve this problem, all of the paint must be removed and the house repainted.

Crawling: This problem can be noticed as the paint job is in progress. Look for little bubbles forming in the fresh paint. The problem can be caused by cold weather or painting when the air is too humid. It can also be the result of poorly mixed paint or the application of paint over an unwashed or greasy surface.

When you spot this taking place, stop and determine which of these problems is the cause.

Wrinkling: This is another problem that can be spotted as painting is in progress. The surface will actually take on the look of a prune. This is usually the result of applying too

6-3
When paint is applied too thick, the effect can be a badly
wrinkled surface.

thick a coat. When a second coat is applied to an undercoat that has not dried sufficiently, the wrinkling will occur. It can also happen when paint is applied to a cold surface on a hot day.

Whatever the cause, stop painting and correct it before you go any further. To solve the problem, use thinner paint and brush it on very well. It may be necessary to remove the wrinkled paint, and to sand the surface before repainting.

Runs and sags: When paint is too thick, you can get a runny, saggy effect. Either brush the thick paint on well, or thin out the paint before proceeding.

Slow drying paint: If the weather was very hot, or very cold, you may have drying troubles with even the best of paints. However, most slow drying is the result of using inexpensive paints. No matter how badly it is applied, a good paint will always dry. But, a badly made paint may never dry. Watch out for bargains in paint. It pays to buy the best—all the time.

Discoloration: Most causes of discoloration come from behind the paint. If knots in the wood were not properly primed before final painting, the resin they contain will stain the paint. It's best to coat these knots with shellac prior to painting.

When metal gutters are near a painted surface, the rain that runs over them onto the painted surface will often discolor the paint. This can be prevented by applying a coat of paint or varnish to the metal.

When a wood surface has creosote stains, it is best to give the stains several coats of shellac before applying paint. Aluminum paint can be used as effectively as shellac.

Mildew: Mildew is actually a fungus that grows on painted surfaces in warm, humid areas. It appears as dark patches of discoloration and is somewhat slimy when you rub a finger through it.

No painting should be started until the surface has been freed of mildew. If you try to paint over mildew, the paint will not adhere properly, and you stand a good chance of spreading the mildew to other parts of the house.

If you have a mildew problem, it's best to use a paint that contains a special chemical that resists the growth of the organism. But, before you apply any paint, all traces of the mildew must be removed. This can best be done by washing the area with a solution made of the following ingredients:

⅓ cup of ordinary household detergent,

⅔ cup of trisodium phosphate (available at paint and hardware stores)

1 quart of chlorine bleach and enough warm water to make up a gallon of the solution.

The affected area should be thoroughly scrubbed down with the cleaner you have made and rinsed well with several applications of fresh water. You should wear rubber gloves when you do the job and wear safety glasses to protect your eyes from splashes.

Don't apply any paint until the surface has dried completely.

Moss: Moss grows on the north side of a tree, as any Boy Scout knows. It also grows on the north side of a house and any place where there is little sun and some moisture. It's pernicious; it grows on and through paint and on just about anything but a highly glossy surface.

There are a number of commercial chemicals available under different brand names that can be used to get rid of moss. But, before you try any of them, give the affected area a thorough going-over with an application of chlorine bleach. Brush it on with a stiff brush and wash away as much of the moss as you can.

It's best to try to brush off the moss during a dry period and then apply a wood preservative such as pentachlorophenol.

Whatever you do to get rid of the moss, the surface must be free of the blight before any paint is applied.

Efflorescence: The white powder that appears on masonry surfaces is called efflorescence. It is the result of moisture meeting the alkalis in the masonry, and it must be treated before any paint is applied.

Use a stiff brush to work in a weak solution of muriatic acid. Scrub the surface vigorously for a few minutes and then flood the area with clear water. Wait until the surface has dried thoroughly before you apply any paint. If you are using a latex paint, you do not have to wait for the surface to dry.

HOW TO PREPARE AN EXTERIOR SURFACE FOR PAINTING

After you have determined the cause of your painting problems, you will have to take steps to correct the situation before you apply any paint. Each of the problems described in the first pages of the chapter tell what should be done. Now, here is *how* to do it.

How to Use Heat to Remove Paint

When severe blistering and other problems dictate that most or all of the paint should be removed, there are several ways of handling the job. The most popular and fastest method is heat. The heat can come from a blowtorch or a propane torch, or from an electric paint scraper. The torch method is quick and effective, but it is very dangerous. In fact, there are some states that prohibit even professional painters from using an open flame to remove paint. Therefore, the method described will be that which uses the electric scraper.

Even an electric scraper can start a fire. Paint can collect in the unit and catch fire, and it is possible to scorch the wood surface if the unit is held in one spot too long. You will need a long, heavy duty extension cord to operate an electric paint scraper over the entire surface of your house.

Just to be safe, have a garden hose nearby. *Don't use the hose on the scraper if collected paint in it catches fire; use the hose on the house if a fire is started.* Unplug the scraper and keep it away from anything that could catch fire. After the paint stops burning, but while it's still soft, peel it from the scraper.

Some electric units are supplied with built-in scrapers.

Other units just soften paint with heat, but require the use of a hand scraper. When you use the latter, simply hold the heating element over the paint until it bubbles. Then, use your scraper to peel the softened paint off the surface.

A word of caution: Be careful when using an electric paint remover near glass. The heat can crack the windows.

There are a variety of different types of hand scrapers you can use. Perhaps the best all-around tools are the 4″ scraper and a putty knife. The 4″ scraper is stiff and good for heavy duty work. The putty knife is flexible and can be used in tight places, such as around molding and windows.

How to Use Chemical Paint Removers

Chemical paint removers are fast and thorough, but they are usually rather expensive and very dangerous to use. They can be flammable and toxic. Be sure to read the label very carefully before you use any of the chemicals. Even if it is 100° in the shade, wear clothes that will cover all of your body, use rubber gloves and be sure to wear safety goggles.

Chemical paint removers are available as liquids or pastes. The liquids are fine for horizontal surfaces, but are not suitable to use on an exterior wall. Therefore, it is best to select a paste or cream chemical paint remover. The creams will stick to the wall while they are doing the job, but they are slower working than the liquids.

There are some chemical paint removers that contain small amounts of wax. This wax is deposited on the surface and must be wiped away with either turpentine or benzine. Other chemical paint removers do not contain any wax and they can be flushed by simply using fresh water. Make sure you know which one you are using.

The best way to apply a chemical paint remover is to use a regular paint brush. Avoid getting any of the chemical on the handle, or you will end up with a sticky mess as the remover works on the finish of the handle. If you have the time, simply sand off the finish on the handle before using the brush to apply the paint remover.

Apply the paste remover with long strokes. Lay down a

thick coat, and do not go back over the paste as you would if you were applying paint. Different removers require different amounts of time to do the job. You can test with your paint scraper; when it's ready you should be able to peel the softened paint off quite easily. Don't rush things; let the paint remover do its job. If you begin scraping before the paint has been thoroughly softened, you may knick the wood and work a lot harder than you have to. In general, most paint removers will do the job in 15 to 20 minutes.

Keep the edge of the scraper clean by wiping it frequently as you work. If the surface you are cleaning has grooves, you can get at the paint with a stiff brush.

It's best to apply the chemical remover to a small area at a time. While one area is being softened, you can be scraping another.

Using a Wire Brush

When the surface does not have to be completely cleared of paint, it is often possible to prepare the surface with a wire brush. The wire brush will loosen and remove chalking, loose paint and much of the accumulated grime. It's best to use a wire brush in conjunction with sandpaper.

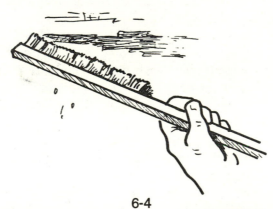

6-4
A wire brush will not only clean a surface, it will roughen it enough to make a fresh coat of paint adhere well.

Using Sandpaper

When small patches of paint have been scraped or brushed off, you should feather the edges of the remaining paint with a piece of sandpaper. Use a coarse sandpaper wrapped around a small block of wood to do the job. Sandpaper should also be used to roughen a smooth surface where fresh paint may not adhere. After using the coarse sandpaper, go over the area with a fine grade of paper or the freshly painted surface may appear rough.

There are power sanders that can be used to remove paint from exterior walls. They are very effective, but somewhat difficult to use. If you want to try one, it might be wise to rent a sander before you consider buying one.

Caulking and Puttying

Before any painting is begun, make sure that all caulking and puttied joints are tight and fresh. Both materials tend to dry and crack. As seasons change, some can contract, leaving cracks where cold air and water can enter the house. As mentioned earlier, water behind the surface is a major cause of most serious paint problems.

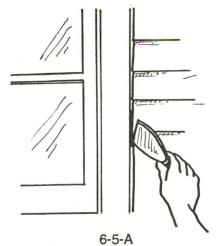

6-5-A
Be sure to remove all dried caulking first.

If you find that some of your window putty has dried, now is the time to replace it. Dig out the old material with your scraper and replace it with fresh putty. It's a good idea to brush on a thin coat of paint primer to the area where the putty will be used. Dry, exposed wood can draw off the oil from the putty and make it dry and brittle before its time.

6-5-B
Apply fresh caulking before any painting is begun

Check all the joints around the house—where walls meet windows, where chimneys meet walls and any other spots that require a seal. If they are open, or if the caulking is dry and brittle, remove it and apply fresh caulking. If you have a fair amount of recaulking to do, it's best to buy a caulking gun and use the handy cartridge packs. It's the least messy and is the easiest way to apply caulking. Smooth the caulking with your putty knife before it sets.

Washing a Surface

After a painted surface has been prepared by scraping, sanding or whatever method is used, it is good to wash it down thoroughly. Accumulated chalk and dust from the sanding and the accumulation of dirt from trees, oil burners and other environmental causes, should be removed. Use a strong household detergent and warm water. Be sure to rinse the surface thoroughly. Wait several days before applying an oil base paint. Latex paints can be applied to a damp surface, but not a wet surface.

How to Cure Staining

If you have any nails that rusted under the old paint, or knots that bled through to the surface, now is the time to take care of them. Nails should be driven into the wood so that their heads are below the surface. Fill the nailhead hole with putty and smooth the putty flat with the surrounding wood.

If resins from wood knots spoiled the previous paint job, you will have to coat them with shellac before applying fresh paint. Let the shellac dry before applying the prime paint coat.

If you detect any cracks in the siding, whether it is a shingle or clapboard, now is the time to take care of the problem. See Chapter 5 for details on these projects.

Until now, I have told you stories of people who have saved considerable money by doing many of their own exterior home repairs. It's true that you can save a lot of money by painting your house yourself, but if you choose the wrong equipment, you can spend two to three times as much time doing the job. One man tried to save money by buying the least expensive brushes he could find. Actually, the brushes he bought were not very dense, and therefore couldn't hold much paint. He had to dip more frequently, and lost some time this way. And the brushes wore down very quickly. He had to replace brushes several times during the job. On several occasions he found himself on a Sunday with an unusable brush. Because the stores in his area were closed on that day, he had some very unproductive weekends. It's smart to be thrifty, but this just wasn't smart. Buy good brushes and you'll do better work in less time than you will with thin, inexpensive brushes.

HOW TO CHOOSE THE RIGHT BRUSH

Earlier I mentioned that you should always buy the best paint; the same goes for the brush. A good brush will make your job a lot easier and you will be able to do a better job.

Generally, all you will need for most exterior painting jobs is a 4″ wall brush and a 1½″ trim brush. The better the brush, the more paint it will hold each time you dip it in the can.

Brush bristles are, for the most part, made of either hog bristle or a synthetic fiber. Even though most of the brushes are made of synthetic materials, I still prefer a brush made of hog bristles. Actually, there probably is very little difference, but the feel of a brush of hog bristle is more comfortable to me.

When you buy your brushes, test a few different brands by fanning the bristles on your forearm. There should be a springiness to the bristles, and they should not fan out excessively. Buy the brush with the most bristles. Obviously you can't count them, but when you look at a number of brushes, you will see that some are more dense than others. Buy the densest brush you can find.

Be sure that the bristles are tightly set in the ferrule— the metal band in the base that holds the bristles in place. Hit the palm of your hand several times with the brush and watch to see if any bristles fall out. You might try tugging on a few selected bristles. They will all come out if you tug hard enough, but a good brush will give you a fight.

You can buy brushes that are cut flat on the bottom or have their bristles cut in a tapered wedge shape. You will find that the wedge shaped brush will make it easier for you to go from one stroke to the next without leaving lap marks.

In addition to the conventional brushes, you can also use some unique and helpful brush substitutes. For latex, there are pads on handles available that make the work go a lot faster and easier. They are great, but it is always a good idea to have a small brush handy to get at the tight spots. Be sure

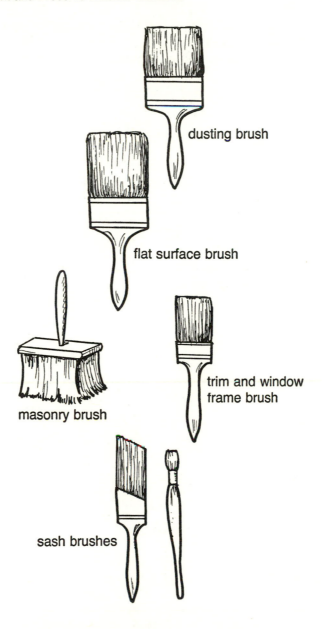

dusting brush

flat surface brush

masonry brush

trim and window
frame brush

sash brushes

6-6
Common brushes used in exterior painting.

to paint the underside of the edge of shingles or clapboard. It's seldom seen and often forgotten.

There are any number of ingenious ways to bring paint to the job. The oldest, and most used, is still the paint hook and the can. When you use the can, you never have to bother cleaning up another container. You just cover the can when you are through for the day, and throw it away when it is empty. However, it's a good idea to look over the equipment at the paint store when you buy your paint. You just might find some unusual equipment that will make what is often a tiresome job a more comfortable one.

HOW TO CARE FOR YOUR BRUSHES

A brush used with latex paint is the easiest to clean. Just hold it under a warm water tap and work out all of the paint. When the water runs clear, your job is done.

6-7
Here's how to clean a paint brush:
1. Soak the brush in the appropriate thinner. Then work the brush against the bottom of the can to loosen paint.

2. Squeeze brush between thumb and forefinger to loosen paint inside bristles.

3. Rinse again in thinner. It often helps to wash the brush in a mild detergent.

4. Twirl the brush in an empty container to shake out the
remaining thinner or water.

5. Wrap the brush in heavy paper and store flat.

A brush used to apply oil or alkyd paints should be
cleaned in turpentine or paint thinner. When all of the paint
has been removed, wash the brush in warm water and a good
household detergent. Be sure to rinse out all of the detergent
before storing the cleaned brush.

A brush used to apply shellac or alcohol based stains
should be cleaned in alcohol, or lacquer thinner. After all of
the shellac or stain has been removed, wash the brush in
warm water and detergent. Rinse the brush thoroughly in
clear water.

When you have completely finished with a brush, clean it
and let it dry. It is a good idea to wrap it for storage in either
heavy brown paper or aluminum foil.

HERE'S WHAT PAINT YOU SHOULD USE

Choose the right paint for the job. Don't be tempted to use up all of the paint that you have left over from other jobs, regardless of what it was used for originally. Use this table to select the proper paint and you will get the best coverage and a paint job that will last a long time.

PAINT SELECTION GUIDE

1. **Aluminum windows**
   Oil base house paint, exterior aluminum paint. Latex paints can also be used, but the surface should be prepared with an appropriate primer.
2. **Asbestos cement walls**
   Exterior latex masonry paint, latex house paint. Oil base house paint can be used, but it should be preceded by an appropriate primer.
3. **Brick**
   Exterior latex masonry paint, latex house paint, transparent sealer, cement base paint.
   Oil base house paint can be used after the application of an appropriate primer.
4. **Concrete block**
   Latex house paint, transparent sealer, cement base paint, exterior aluminum paint.
   Exterior masonry latex and oil base house paints can also be used after a primer.
5. **Concrete porch or patio**
   Porch and deck enamel, some latex paints (read labels).
6. **Copper gutters**
   Spar varnish.
7. **Galvanized metal**
   Spar varnish. After an appropriate primer, these paints can be used: Latex house paint, oil base house paint, exterior aluminum paint, latex and oil trim paints.
8. **Iron**
   The following paints can be used on iron surfaces after the

---

application of an appropriate primer: latex house paint, oil base house paint, exterior aluminum paint, oil and latex trim paints.

9. **Metal roofs**
   After the application of an appropriate primer, oil base and latex house paints can be used.
10. **Metal siding**
    Latex house paint. The following paints can be applied after an appropriate primer: oil base house paint, exterior aluminum paint.
11. **Natural wood siding and trim**
    Wood stain, exterior clear finishes, spar varnish.
12. **Steel windows**
    Apply an appropriate primer before using these paints: latex house paint, oil base house paint, exterior aluminum paint, latex and oil base trim paint.
13. **Shutters, wood**
    After priming, use these paints: latex house paint, oil base house paint, latex and oil base trim paint.
14. **Stucco**
    Exterior masonry latex paint, latex house paint, transparent sealer, cement base paint, exterior aluminum paint. An oil base paint can be used, but a primer should be applied first.
15. **Wood window frames**
    After a primer, use latex house paint, oil base house paint, and oil or latex trim paint. Exterior aluminum paint can be used without a primer.
16. **Wood shingled roof**
    Wood stain.
17. **Wood porch deck**
    Porch and deck enamel.
18. **Wood siding**
    Latex or oil base house paint. Use a primer before applying oil base house paint.

Note: This table should serve only as a general guide. It is best to check carefully with your paint dealer if you have any special or unusual conditions.

HERE'S THE ORDER IN WHICH TO PAINT
THE OUTSIDE OF YOUR HOUSE

Start with the walls first. Then do the trim and follow this with the porches and decks. Be sure to remove shutters before painting them. They are usually painted a color which is different from the house, and you don't want to drip red paint on freshly painted white clapboard.

Start your painting at the top of the house. Work across and down in sections that are most comfortable for you. If you are painting from a single ladder, you will have to move it frequently to get the coverage; don't try to reach too far, or you might unbalance the ladder and fall. When using scaffolding, the job is a lot easier.

Be sure to use a dropcloth to protect anything under the area you are painting. You should even cover your bushes. You may think that a few drops of paint won't harm the leaves. But think of what might happen if the entire can plopped on your prize rose bush.

The best time of year to paint is in the spring and fall. The weather is usually stable during these seasons, and there are enough leaves on the trees to keep away the direct sunlight. Don't paint too late in the fall, or you might have a lot of falling leaves stick to your fresh paint.

You can paint in the hot weather, but don't apply paint in the hot sun. Paint the west side of the house in the morning when the sun is rising and the east side of the house in the afternoon. Try to wait for a cloudy day to do the south side when it is hit by sun all day. The north side can be painted anytime, but be sure to check for moss and fungus before you get started.

Follow the suggestions in the table for the proper paint to use and be sure to use a primer where one is required. If you are not repainting, but are applying paint to new work, you must apply the primer which the manufacturer of the finish paint recommends.

HOW TO APPLY PAINT TO SIDING

When you have selected the paint and the brush and have properly prepared the surface, you are ready. Begin by mixing the paint thoroughly, even though it might have been mixed at the paint store. Paint can settle quickly, and if you apply it in this state, you will have uneven color coverage and a number of other problems.

As I mentioned earlier, use the can to hold the paint while you work. The brush should be dipped into the paint so that about one-third of it picks up paint. Gently wipe one side of the brush against the rim as you withdraw it from the can.

When painting clapboard and other horizontal siding, paint the underside of the boards first. Cover these projecting areas in the area you are painting and then paint the surface of the boards. The paint should be applied along the length of the siding in long back-and-forth strokes. Take care to smooth out overlapping strokes and any drips from the board above. It is best to finish a course of siding before starting on the next course below. If you are using latex paint, it really doesn't matter if you don't finish a complete board before proceeding to another below it. There is less tendency for latex to show lap marks.

When painting shingles, you will have to paint up and down, if there is any deep surface grain. Follow the same general procedure outlined for the painting of clapboard, with the following exceptions.

HOW TO PAINT EVERYTHING ELSE OUTSIDE THE HOUSE

Gutters

Before any gutter is painted, you should make sure that it is working properly and is not clogged. If the gutter has sagged, it may not carry off the water to the downspout, and an overflow could stain the side of the house. The outside of the gutters are usually painted at the same time as the rest of the house. But read on for specific types of gutters.

Copper gutters are seldom painted. They are usually left to turn brown from weathering. However, when water drips from a copper gutter, it can stain the side of the house. You may want to apply a coat of spar varnish. If you decide to apply a pigmented paint, it's best to use a good grade of exterior trim enamel.

Aluminum gutters are usually supplied with a factory-applied finish. This surface seldom needs painting, but when it does, the surface must be roughened with sandpaper before any paint can be applied. Then it is possible to use the same paint that is being used on the exterior trim.

Galvanized steel gutters will rust quickly if they are not protected. It's best to apply a thick coat of asphalt roofing cement to the inside to prevent this problem. The exterior of the gutter can be painted with conventional exterior paint.

Wood gutters will last a long time, if they are properly tended. The outside of the gutter can be painted with the exterior paint that you are using for the rest of the house, but the inside should be coated with either asphalt roofing cement or regular applications of linseed oil. If the gutter is new and being painted for the first time, apply a liberal coating of a paintable wood preservative first. A once-a-year application of linseed oil to all of the internal surfaces will keep wood gutters in top shape for years. But make sure the gutters are thoroughly dry before you apply the oil.

Porches and Decks

Wood porches and decks should be painted with a good grade of deck enamel. A wood porch and deck is hard to keep painted. Dampness is constantly getting into the wood to force the paint off, and the normal scuffing of feet wears the paint thin quickly.

A pigmented exterior oil stain is a better choice to protect a wood deck, or porch. This material works into the wood, and does not lay on the surface as does paint. It won't peel or blister. You can buy exterior oil stains with a heavy or light pigmentation, depending on how much of the wood you want to hide. Be sure that the wood is dry before applying this finish.

If you are building a porch, it is best to apply the stain to the boards before the porch is built. This way, all surfaces of the wood will have the protection offered by the finish. If the porch has already had a coat of paint, you will have to remove all of the paint before applying a fresh coat of oil stain. At this point, it is usually wiser to simply apply a fresh coat of deck paint.

HOW TO
FIX ANYTHING THAT
CAN GO WRONG
WITH WINDOWS,
SCREENS AND
STORM WINDOWS

Why an entire chapter on windows? Think for a moment just how important windows are. In the winter, they keep the snow out and the heat in. In summer they keep the rain out and the cool in. Like most other small things, we often take windows for granted and forget that even a small air leak can add up to extra fuel bills in winter and a higher electric bill in the summer for air conditioning. And a stuck window is just a plain pain when you want to air the house.

I was told of a man who compared his fuel bill with that of his neighbor. They each had the same type of house, and both kept their winter temperature set at the same point. However, one of them was paying almost 20 percent more in fuel bills. At first, he thought that he was having trouble with his furnace, but a professional inspection showed that there were no problems. Further investigation led this man to discover that most of his storm windows were a little loose, and some of his double-hung windows were sticky enough so that they couldn't be fully closed. At first he thought that these few leaks could not account for his heat losses, but when he fixed them, his fuel bills went down to the same level as those of his neighbor. One little leak isn't much, but if you add up all of the area of all of the little leaks, you can get a clear picture of why your heating bills can skyrocket if you neglect window maintenance.

Obviously, windows deserve attention and this chapter will cover the major types of windows in enough detail so that you will be able to get the most from them and enjoy trouble-free use.

Windows are made of many materials, and are produced in a number of different styles. Wood is probably the most common material, but many homes and apartments are now being built with aluminum or steel windows. Each has its advantages and disadvantages—there is no one window that is best for every house.

In addition to the permanent windows in your home, the chances are good that you have storm windows and screens as well. There is hardly a house that could not benefit from a set of storm windows in the winter, and screens in summer.

To make window repair and maintenance as easy as possible, I have divided this chapter into sections which cover every major type of window. Let's begin with the most common wood window—double-hung.

THE DOUBLE-HUNG WINDOW

The double-hung window is, perhaps, the most popular architectural choice for a window. With a number of lights (panels of glass) it can be used nicely in a colonial design. With single panes of glass, the window will look well in just about any other style. Most double-hung windows are made of wood, but there are some models that are made of metal.

The name of the window is derived from the two sections hung in the frame. The upper section is on the outside and the lower section on the inside. When both sections are closed, there is usually a latch on the top rail of the lower sash to lock the two sashes together.

To keep the windows in place, whether closed or open to any position, there are two systems. One system uses a set of weights attached by rope or chain to the sash. The weights are hidden in the wall behind the side jambs, and act to counterbalance the window. The other system uses a set of springs mounted in tubes which are positioned on either side of the sash on the side jambs. The tension on the spring is adjustable to compensate for variations in the windows.

A third system is used primarily to replace a broken sash

7-1
The conventional double-hung window.

weight system. Rather than take the window apart to fix a broken sash weight balance system, the sash balance fits in where the pulley had been mounted, and attaches to the sash without any difficulty. This system acts like a tape measure; as it is pulled out, a spring is wound to create tension.

How to Fix a Sticking Double-Hung Window

Double-hung windows stick for a number of reasons, and each problem is easy to correct. The most obvious problem is caused by paint which has joined the sash to the rest of the window. Don't try to force the window; you can damage it, and you will probably pull off paint at the spots where the window is sticking. The best approach is to free the sash carefully by prying a wide paint scraper between the stops and the sash until the window has been loosened. Position the scraper at the stuck joint and tap the handle lightly with a hammer until you have penetrated the paint. Move the scraper along the sash until all of the paint has been loosened.

7-2
You can break a paint seal with a paint scraper
and a hammer.

If you find any lumps of paint on the parting strip (the strip of wood that separates the two sashes) either trim them down with a knife or razor blade, or sand them flat so that when the sashes are moved up or down, they won't be hindered.

If paint has accumulated in the grooves formed by the stops, the windows will be difficult to operate. Usually, the problem can be solved by sanding down the painted surfaces until the window works smoothly. Incidentally, when you paint, use well-thinned paint in the grooves to prevent the problem of paint build-up.

Some window sticking problems are transient. That is, when the weather gets moist and sticky, the windows stick. This is the result of the wood taking in water and swelling to the point where the windows no longer fit and slide easily. You can do a little sanding, but don't take away too much wood. When the weather dries, the windows will be loose and drafty. The best bet is to apply some lubrication on the edges of the inside and blind stops as well as to both sides of the parting strip. There are some silicone lubricants made specifically for this job, but if you can't find them, you can do just as good a job with a lump of paraffin or hard soap. Just rub on enough to make the windows slide smoothly.

If these steps fail, there is no other recourse; you will have to remove the sashes and plane them lightly until they slide freely. To remove the sashes, it is only necessary to pry off the inside stop on one side. You will be able to lift out the lower sash with this stop removed. To remove the upper sash, pry out the parting strip on the same side. You will be able to swing the upper sash free. When you have these windows freed, they will still be tethered by the rope or chain that attaches them to the sash weights. Be sure to secure the sash cords to something or they may fall behind the side jamb.

Before you do any sanding or planing on the sash, sand the surfaces of the inside stop and the parting strip. Test for movement with the sashes and stops in place. If this does the job, remove the inside stop and parting strip on the other side and sand or plane off the same amount of wood or accumulated paint. When you are certain that you have removed enough, reassemble the window and apply a thinned coat of paint over spots that have gotten down to the wood.

If the sash sticks between the stiles and the jambs, plane off enough sash surface to restore easy movement. Do this planing in small steps, testing the fit as you go. You don't want to take away too much wood or the windows will rattle and let in the weather.

Lubricating a Double-Hung Window

Even if you don't have sticking problems, it is a good idea to occasionally lubricate the sliding surfaces of your double-hung windows. Don't overdo it, but an occasional rubbing of paraffin over the stops and the parting strip will keep things moving nicely.

How to Replace a Sash Cord

When sash weights are hung with rope, you can be sure that a time will come when the lines will part and you will be faced with a window that doesn't work. When this happens, don't just replace the broken rope, replace both of them—with a sash chain.

Begin this job by removing the inside stop molding. Most windows have several coats of paint on them by the time a sash cord parts, so, to prevent a lot of cracked paint, use a sharp knife to cut all the edges where the stop meets the frame.

7-3-A
Remove the inside stop on one side.

When the stop molding has been removed, pull the side of the sash nearest the exposed jamb slightly forward and then slide the window clear of the frame. Remove the remaining section of sash cord. This cord is secured in a channel and held by a plain knot. Just pulling the cord from the channel and easing it from the hole at the end is all that is required.

Next, you will have to get at the sash weight. Windows are made in two ways, and you will have to determine which method was used to make your windows before you can get at the weight. Some windows have little doors fitted right into the lower portion of the side jamb. Even if your jamb has a number of coats of paint, you should still be able to see the outline of the door. Use a sharp knife to slice through the paint around the door, and chip away at the paint to uncover the screw at the bottom that holds it in place. When you remove the screw, you will be able to pry the door loose from the bottom. It holds by being tucked in on the top. With the

7-3-B
If you don't have a pry bar, the stop can be lifted with a paint scraper.

7-3-C
In some windows, the sash weight is located behind a little door at the bottom of the lower sash.

door open, you will have access to the weights and can remove them in order to attach a sash chain.

If your window does not have such a sash door, it will be necessary to remove the frame, or side casing, in order to get at the sash weight. Again, score the painted joints with a knife to prevent chipping and simply pry the frame free.

Whichever way your window was made, you should now be in a position to remove the sash weight. Measure the two

7-3-D
Remove the cover and lift out the sash weight.

pieces of the parted sash rope and cut a piece of chain to the same total length. Feed the end of the chain over the pulley and lower it until it is visible through the jamb door and can be pulled out a few inches. You can put a nail or a paper clip through the link nearest the pulley to prevent the chain from falling into the frame.

Pull out enough chain through the door to allow you to attach it to the hole in the sash weight. Use several turns of fairly heavy wire to secure the links that have been fed through the hole in the weight to the rest of the chain. After all, you don't want a repeat performance as a result of a loosened wire.

When the weight has been firmly attached, connect the

other end of the chain to the sash. You can do this by driving a wood screw through one of the links and into the back of the slot in the sash that had held the rope.

7-3-E
After the stop has been removed, swing one side
of the window free.

7-3-F
Free the sash cord from the well cut in the sash stile. It is
held in place with a knot.

After you have tested your repair and found that it works properly, replace the door, or the frame molding, and the job is done.

If all you are doing is replacing the cords on the upper sash, it is still necessary to remove the lower sash. In addition, you will remove the parting strip that guides the upper sash.

How to Install a Sash Balance

If you thought that all that rigamarole described in the last repair was more than you care to tackle, take heart. You can solve the problem without having to do any removal of wood, and you can leave the old sash weight right in the frame and forget about it.

The little device that solves this problem resembles a tape measure, and it fits into the hole occupied by the pulley. Just remove the screws holding the pulley and slip the spring-loaded sash balance in its place and secure it with screws.

The tape that pulls out of the balance is attached to an L-shaped bracket which is simply screwed to the top of the

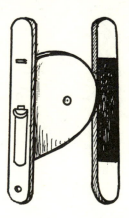

7-4-A
A sash balance is designed to fit in the space occupied by
the original sash pulley.

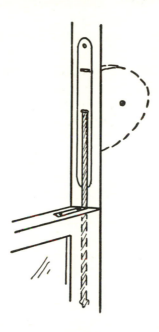

7-4-B
Pull out the tape and attach it to the window. A special
adaptor is supplied with the sash balance to be attached
to the window.

lower sash. The hook part of the bracket, along with the tape from the balance, is fitted to the groove occupied by the rope.

It's a simple, fast and effective way of solving your sash weight problems.

How to Adjust a Spring-Lift Window

If your window doesn't have the weight and pulley balance, it is probably controlled by a spring-loaded tube system. To determine if this is the type of window you have, look between the stops and see if there is a tube mounted on both side jambs. Inside this tube is a spring, and, over the years, it can loose its tension and require adjustment.

To either increase or decrease the spring tension, first remove the screw at the top that holds the tube in place.

When the screw has been removed from the jamb, keep it in the tube and hold it firmly.

If you find it difficult to raise the window, increase the tension on the spring by winding on two or three more turns. If the window creeps up, you will want to reduce the tension. To do this, unwind the spring two or three turns.

In either case, replace the tube and test your repair. It might require additional turns to do the job.

These windows can also benefit from an occasional application of a lubricant such as paraffin to the stops and parting strip.

How to Replace Glass in a Wood Sash

When glass breaks in an area that could be dangerous—near where someone sits, etc.—it is best to replace it with safety glass, or one of the new plastics. The latter is better for yet another reason; it is a lot more difficult for a burglar to get into a house when the windows are plastic than when they are made of glass.

Before you can replace glass, it is first necessary to remove all the broken shards. Be sure to wear heavy work gloves when you do this.

After all the pieces of glass have been removed, the next step is to get rid of the old putty. If it is dry enough, you can

7-5-A
Remove all broken glass. Protect your hand with
a work glove.

7-5-B
Remove the dried putty.

probably pick it away with a putty knife or a screwdriver. But be careful not to dig into the wood sash. If the putty is especially resistant to your efforts, it can be softened with a soldering iron, or a gas torch that has a soldering attachment. When the putty has been softened, it can be removed more easily.

When all the old putty has been cleaned out, remove the glazer's points (little metal triangles used to position the glass) and sand the groove well. Brush away the sanding dust and then coat all four grooves with some thinned exterior paint or linseed oil. This will prevent the wood from absorbing the oil from the new putty when the job is done.

Measure the opening, but have the replacement glass cut about ⅛ inch shorter in both the length and width. This will

7-5-C
Lay a thin bed of putty around the frame to
cushion the glass.

allow for expansion and any irregularities and make it a lot easier to do the job. Don't worry about air leaks; this glass will be firmly sealed with glazer's putty.

Before you position the new pane, lay a thin bed of putty along all four sides to act as a cushion. This step will also help to prevent stress on the sash from cracking the glass.

Position the new pane, hold it in place and set it with glazer's points. These little wedges should be set every four

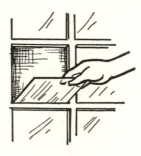

7-5-D
Position the new piece of glass.

to six inches around the entire pane. To use them, position one of the points toward the sash and hold it flat against the pane of glass. With the little tool that is packed with some points, or with the blade of a screwdriver and a light hammer, tap these points into the sash about half way. Do this job gingerly; you can break the glass. Hold the screwdriver blade flat against the flat side of the point. The screwdriver should be almost parallel to the glass so that none of the hammer taps will be transmitted to the glass.

When all the points are set, roll some putty in your hand to form a long tube about the size of the area to be filled. Use your forefinger to press the putty into the groove around the entire window. When the groove has been filled, use the corner of a putty knife to flatten and form the putty. Follow the same angle as the putty in the other windows. If the corner of the blade is held against the glass and the knife is drawn slowly over each groove, the putty should form nicely.

7-5-E
Set the glass with glazer's points. A simple setter wedge is
often included with a box of points.

Any excess will be squeezed away and it can be picked off
after the smoothing has been finished. If more putty is
needed, just press it in place and work it in with the putty
knife.

7-5-F
Reputty the window over the glazer's points.

The job is done—except for the painting. But this should
be done after the putty has dried. Wait a week or so and then
do the job. It's best to overlap the paint on the glass a tiny
distance. This will prevent rain from getting behind the putty
and doing damage to the sash.

7-5-G
Smooth the putty with a clean putty knife.

How to Cut Glass

If you have glass and want to cut a replacement piece from it, it's an easy job. But, it should be done with care. You don't worry about damaging the glass—you worry about yourself. I don't have to tell you that some very bad cuts can result from mishandling glass. As suggested for removing the broken glass, it's a good idea to wear heavy gloves when you cut glass. Safety glasses will prevent chips from getting in your eyes if you have an accident.

To cut glass, you will need an ordinary glass cutter, a good straight edge, pliers, some kerosene or turpentine and a perfectly flat surface.

You can mark the line to be cut with a grease pencil. After the line has been marked, cover it with a wipe of turpentine or kerosene. Hold the straight edge tightly against the line and make a firm score with the little wheel on the glass cutter. Once the glass has been scored, place the section to be removed—the waste part—past the edge of a table. Make sure that the table is flat. Hold the part of the glass that is on the table firmly and lightly tap the extending glass with a gloved hand. It will probably snap right off and leave a perfectly even cut. But if it doesn't, you might not have scored deeply enough. No matter; just grip the waste portion in the middle *lightly* with the pliers and snap off the piece.

Glass is quite easy to work with, once you get the hang of it. You might want to experiment on some old pieces before you tackle a good piece.

How to Weatherstrip a Double-Hung Window

A lot of costly heat leaks to the outside when windows are not properly sealed. To solve this problem, there are many different types of weatherstripping now being made. Rather than describe every type, it would be best for you to look at what is available at your local hardware store and decide for yourself, or with the help of the clerk. However, there are some types of weatherstripping that have been in use for years, and that would be worth knowing about.

There is a spring metal weatherstripping that is nailed in each sash channel. Only one side is nailed down; the other side springs up and makes contact with the sash stile to seal leaks. No need to remove the windows to install this weatherstrip-

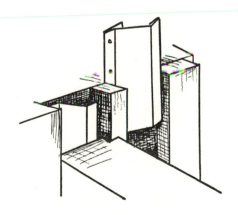

7-6-A
Spring metal insulation is fitted directly between the window
stile and the side jamb.

ping. Just raise the lower sash to its greatest height, slip the end of the strip up under the sash, and position the strip so that it contacts the sill. Use small wire brads to hold the strip in place.

To weatherstrip the upper sash, lower it all the way, and repeat the process in reverse.

The same spring stripping can be nailed to the lower rail on the bottom sash to seal drafts between it and the sill.

When the window is closed, there is always a little space between the top rail of the lower sash and the bottom rail of

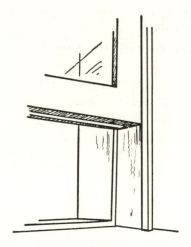

7-6-B
Nail a piece of spring metal insulation along the full width
of the window.

the upper sash. This space can also be protected by the installation of a strip of spring insulation.

In all cases, use a countersink to recess the heads of the brads slightly. If they stick out, they can make it difficult to use the window.

If your only problem is a leak where the bottom rail of the lower sash meets the sill, it can be fixed easily with one of the many types of self-sticking insulations. Just raise the window,

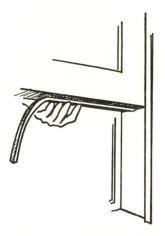

7-7
Remove the protective covering, and apply the self-adhesive
foam insulation to the bottom of the window.

peel the protective backing from the insulation and stick it to
the bottom of the rail. This material is usually very compressible and will seldom prevent the window from closing completely.

Other types of weatherstripping can be mounted where
the sash meets the stops, but there are so many types that,
rather than give specific instructions, it is best to follow the
directions packed with each type. None are particularly difficult to install and all work quite well.

THE CASEMENT WINDOW

Many apartments and homes have been built with casement windows. Mounted in metal frames, the window sash is
also made of metal. Because of the metal construction, casement windows seldom need repairs, but adjustments are
more often required.

The casement window is hinged to the frame, and it is
opened and closed by a crank mechanism which operates a

slide connected to the sash. As the crank is turned, the slide either pushes the window out or closes it, and here is where some of the trouble can occur with this type of window. If anything collects in the frame to make it difficult to close the window, there is often a tendency to force the crank to get a tight closure. This can work as long as the debris can be compressed enough by the window to make a seal. But, as more and more debris accumulates, more force on the handle and the gear mechanism will be required. Often, the spline on the crankshaft will be stripped by the force, and the crank will no longer turn the shaft.

To prevent this from happening, it is a good idea to brush out the casement frames at least once a week. As long as the windows close tightly with very little effort, everything is OK.

How to Lubricate the Closing Mechanism

The gear drive operator is usually mounted with several screws to the bottom of the frame, and can be taken off by removing the screws. Once the operator is free of the frame, move the slide back and forth until it disengages from the track. Draw the slide through the slot which is behind the operator, and you have the entire assembly in your hand, ready for inspection, cleaning and lubrication.

Check the gear and crank mechanism from the back, noting if any parts are broken or worn. If the inside of the operator is gunked up, flush out the debris with a solvent such as benzine. Once the works have been cleaned and are dry, apply a liberal amount of ordinary automobile grease or white petroleum jelly to all of the moving parts. This includes the track in which the slide moves.

If you have any broken parts, you can try to find replacements, but it is probably going to be less of a bother to replace the entire operator. Getting the replacement parts can be a problem, and doing the repair job can be sticky.

After you have remounted the operator, apply a few drops of light oil to the crank handle shaft and to all of the window hinges. Open and close the window several times to work in the grease and to distribute the oil on the shaft. With all of the moving parts thoroughly lubricated, the window should operate freely, but if there still is some resistance, check for binding where the slide passes through the window frame and where it is attached to the sash. Often, a slight bend will eliminate binding at these points and leave the window in top shape.

Rust can be a problem with casement windows, and you should be sure that all the metal is thoroughly painted. Any rust that finds its way into the moving parts of the hinges or the operator will make it difficult to open or close the window.

How to Weatherstrip a Casement Window

If, in spite of your cleaning, the window just doesn't close tightly enough to keep out the drafts, the best move is to apply some weatherstripping. The best material for this task is the foam which is backed with a self-adhesive material. Locate the area that leaks, and apply the stripping to the frame. As the window is closed, it will compress the weatherstripping and eliminate the air leaks.

How to Replace Glass in a Casement Window

Glass is replaced in a casement window in much the same way as it is in a double-hung window, except that the glazer's points are replaced by little wire springs which hold the pane to the sash.

Begin by removing all the remaining broken glass. Be sure to wear work gloves when you do this to protect your hands. When the glass has been removed, use a knife or a small chisel to clear out all of the dried putty and other debris. You should save the spring clips that you have removed; they will be used to position the new pane.

After the sash has been brushed thoroughly, apply a light coat of paint to prevent rusting. When the paint has dried, apply a light bead of glazing compound evenly around the entire frame. This will serve to cushion the glass; it should not be set directly against the metal frame.

Position the new glass and press it firmly into the bed of glazing compound. Use the spring clips by fitting them to the

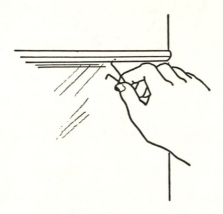

7-8
Spring clips act like glazer's points to hold glass in place
in casement window.

holes in the frame to hold the new glass in place. When all of the springs have been positioned, apply a layer of compound to the outside of the glass. Use a putty knife to smooth the compound to the same contour as the putty in the other windows. In a week or so the compound should be dry, and it will be safe to apply a coat of paint. Overlap the paint about $1/16$ inch on the glass to seal against moisture.

STORM WINDOWS

In colder climates, storm windows are often fitted over existing windows for additional protection against the weather. Most of the new storm windows are being made with aluminum frames, and they generally are combination storm and screen windows. Wood frame storm windows must be removed before screens can be installed, but with the combination windows, it is a simple matter to slide the storm section up and pull down the screen. And there is no storage problem as there is with separate wood frame storm windows and screens.

When properly installed, storm windows can help cut fuel bills and make a house much more comfortable to live in. But, as with anything else in the house, you can have problems here. First, let's look at a problem that can be common to both aluminum and wood frame storm windows.

How to Prevent Condensation

During the winter, if you notice condensation on the inside of the house window which is protected by a storm window, the chances are good that there is air leakage someplace around the storm window. Cold air is getting past the storm window and contacting the outside surface of the house window. When the glass is cold, the inside surface will cause condensation to occur because of the warm inside air.

Obviously, you must seek out and stop the air leak in the storm window. If you have an aluminum window, it was probably installed with screws and sealed to the frame with putty or caulking compound. Check the entire perimeter and seal any leaks that you find. Because wood frame windows are removed at the end of the winter season, they are not sealed with putty. If they have become loose, add some weatherstripping to the leaking points and you will have solved the problem. The best weatherstripping to use here is the foam material supplied with a self-adhesive backing. Just peel off the protective tape and apply the strip to seal the joint.

If you find moisture collecting on the inside surface of the storm window, it is probably because warm air is leaking from the house to the space between the house and storm window. ·First, check to make sure that the house window is closed tightly. If it is closed, but there are spaces where the warm air can escape, you will have to apply an appropriate form of weatherstripping to the house window to prevent the warm air leak.

It may seem silly, but storm windows can be a big help in the summer. If you have an air conditioner in a room with windows that are seldom, if ever, opened in the summer, leave the storms on. They can help the air conditioner to run more efficiently.

How to Replace Glass in a Wood Storm Window

Wood frame storm windows are glazed in the same fashion as a regular double-hung window. See the instructions for this repair to solve this problem.

How to Strengthen Wobbly Storm Windows

When the joints of a storm window open, the window will become rickety, and it can be dangerous to handle such a window. If the frame is in particularly bad shape, it is possible for it to come apart in your hands during the seasonal change. And you know the dangers of a piece of glass at the top of a ladder.

The joints are easy to fix. First, pry the joint open just enough so that you can insert a thin knife blade. Use the blade to scrape away the dry glue. Then apply fresh glue and use

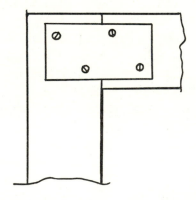

7-9-A
A metal mending plate can be used to reinforce corners.

the blade to spread it over the inside of the joint. Before the glue begins to set, force the joint together, and reinforce it with a metal mending plate. This will not only hold the joint tightly while the glue sets, it will add more reinforcement to the joint. If you want to do the job quickly, skip the metal mending plate and screws and simply drive a corrugated wave dowel across the glued joint.

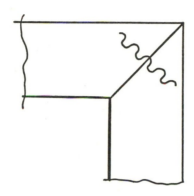

7-9-B
A mitered joint can be reinforced with a wave dowel.

How to Replace Glass in an Aluminum Storm Window

The panes in aluminum storm windows are mounted in aluminum frames that must be disassembled. Some frames snap together and others are held in place with small screws. Whatever system you have, handle the frame with the broken glass very carefully. Pick out the broken glass with a gloved hand, and then disassemble one side of the frame. Measure the perimeter of the inside track, and buy a piece of replacement glass that is about 1/16″ smaller on all sides. Before installing the new pane, it should be surrounded by a protective gasket. The type of gasket depends upon the window, and the chances are that you can use the old gasket if you removed the broken glass carefully. With some windows, the gasket is installed after the glass is positioned in the frame.

Reassemble the aluminum frame, replace the sash, and the job is done.

JALOUSIE WINDOWS

This is the window that looks like a glass Venetian blind. It is made of a series of glass slats mounted in a frame which can be opened and closed by turning a crank in the frame. Generally speaking, these windows are found in warmer climates because it is pretty difficult to get a complete seal. With all of the glass and all of the moving parts, there are bound to be places where the air is going to leak in.

How to Stop Leaks in Jalousie Windows

Don't force individual sections to get a tighter seal; the chances are good that you will stop one air leak, but open another. The best remedy is to apply one of the transparent weatherstripping materials.

How to Replace Glass in Jalousie Windows

Each glass slat is held in place at the ends in individual frames. To remove the glass, simply bend the retaining clips back just enough to permit the glass to slide free. However, if the glass has been broken, the chances are good that all of the

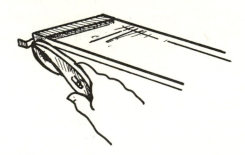

7-10-A
Bend the clips to allow the glass to be removed.

glass shards will have fallen free. But, it will be necessary to bend the clip just enough to allow you to slip in a piece of replacement glass. When the glass is in place, bend the clips back to hold it in place. You can use pliers to do the job, but be careful not to crimp the clip and crack the glass.

7-10-B
Slide replacement glass in place, and then bend retaining clips back in place.

How to Lubricate Jalousie Windows

There are a lot of moving parts in a jalousie window and, unless they are lubricated occasionally, they will become increasingly difficult to operate in time. A drop or two of light oil at all the pivot points on both sides of the glass slats as well as on the operating shaft attached to the crank will go a long way toward preventing problems.

Maintenance of Jalousie Windows

When anything gets stuck between the slats of a jalousie window, any force on the crank to close it can crack glass or damage the operating mechanism. It's a good idea to check the edges of the slats before you close a jalousie just to make sure that nothing will prevent full closure. Just brush the slats once in a while to prevent problems.

AWNING WINDOWS

An awning window is hinged from the top and is opened and closed by a crank mechanism, or held in place by a notched slide on one side. These windows are made of metal as well as wood, and glass should be replaced in the same manner as described for casement or double-hung wood windows in this chapter.

Occasional lubrication of the crank and lift mechanism with light oil will keep the windows working smoothly, and they can be sealed from bad weather by the addition of the self-adhering type of weatherstripping.

Because awning windows open out, they can be kept open in all but the most driving rain. Screens must be mounted on the inside, but this makes it easy to install and remove them when necessary.

SCREENS

Screens have been made of just about every imaginable material. Fortunately, they are no longer made of enameled steel wire. This is the material that would rust and, in a rain storm, the rust would run down the side of a nicely painted house. Now, screening is made of metals such as aluminum, copper, bronze and brass; also, much screening is being made of different plastic materials.

Basic Maintenance of Wood Screen Frames

Wood screen frames should be kept painted. This is not just for aesthetic purposes; it is important to prevent moisture from getting into the wood. If the screen frame absorbs water, it will expand and become difficult to install or remove. When a swollen screen is forced into a window frame, you can damage the paint on the frame.

If the joints become loose, you should re-glue them, and add some form of mechanical protection. A conventional mending plate or a corrugated dowel positioned across the joint will help keep the joints tight. You can also drive a wood screw through the joint, but be sure to countersink the head so that it will not interfere with mounting. After the screw is in place, fill the hole with putty and paint over it.

Basic Maintenance of Aluminum Screen Frames

Aluminum screen frames that are assembled with sheet metal screws can loosen after a while. It's just a matter of retightening the screws to put the frame back in shape. But . . . don't overtighten; it's easy to strip the threads that have been cut in the aluminum by the self-tapping screws that are often used. If this happens, you will either have to reposition the screw nearby, or use a larger screw in the old hole.

The surface of the aluminum should be cleaned with a scouring cleanser and waxed occasionally to prevent oxidation.

How to Patch Small Holes in Metal and Plastic Screening

A small hole is one which can be pressed together easily, but requires something to hold the ends of the wire or plastic together. Use ordinary white waterproof glue to seal such a hole in metal screening and a solvent based glue for plastic. If you reassemble the ends carefully, and use a minimum of glue, the mend will be almost invisible.

How to Repair a Large Hole in Metal Screening

Large holes in metal screening can be repaired by making a patch. Cut the patch from the same metal used to make the screen, but make it about an inch larger on all sides. Next, pull strands from each side of the patch so that the wire going in the opposite direction is exposed for about ½″. Fold these strands down on all four sides evenly and position the patch over the hole. Push the strands through the screen and bend them over on the other side. When you bend the wire, back up the screen with something flat, such as a piece of board. This

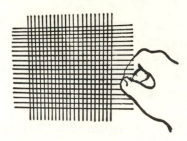

7-11-A
Make a screen patch by removing wire from each side of a
piece of screening that will be big enough to cover the hole.

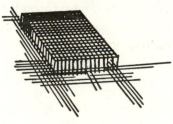

7-11-B
Fold the free wires down and force them through the screen.
Bend the wire over on the opposite side.

will prevent you from stretching the screen when you press
the ends of the patch wires down firmly. Press the edges of
the section of torn screen flat against the patch and trim away
any loose wire. Apply a coat of thin varnish over the patch
and hole and the job is done.

How to Repair a Large Hole in Plastic Screening

A large hole in plastic screening can be repaired in much
the same way as was just described for metal screening.
However, you will not be able to bend the ends of the patch as
was done with the wire. After you have made the patch by
stripping strands from all four sides, push the strands
through the screen around the hole, but secure the patch by
gluing the threads in place.

How to Repair a Gash in Metal and Plastic Screening

A long gash, as compared with a punched-out hole, can often be repaired in much the same fashion as sewing a tear in a piece of fabric. First, close the gash and position the ends as neatly as possible. Then, using a piece of the metal or plastic that was used in the construction of the screen, proceed to sew the hole closed. Thread the wire or plastic back and forth across the gash, but be careful not to pull too hard; you can dislodge the surrounding wire and make a bigger hole than you already have.

This weaving is the first step. Once the hole has been closed, use glue to finish the job. Obviously, the patch job will not be as strong as the screen was before the damage, but it will keep out the bugs.

How to Replace Screen in a Wood Frame

When the holes are not repairable, it's best to replace the entire section of screening. To remove screening from a wood frame, you first have to pry up the molding that has been tacked on all four sides of the screen. Do this with a putty knife or a wide paint scraper—and do it gently. You will have to replace this molding when the new screen is in place.

When the molding has been removed, take out the old screening. The material was probably stapled or tacked around the frame. Be sure to remove all of the staples or tacks.

Even if all of your screens have the old enameled steel screen, do the replacement job with one of the new rustproof metal or plastic materials. Buy the screening several inches larger on all sides, and do not trim away the excess until it has been tacked in place.

Begin by stapling or tacking only one end of the screen. The screen should be tight and, in order to make sure of this, you should bend the frame slightly. Even with two people, this can be a tough job. The best way to get a bow in the screen is to put two pieces of wood about two inches thick under either end on a flat table. Then, use two C-clamps in the middle on both sides to pull the center of the screen down to the table level. This will provide sufficient bend so that when the screen is installed, and the clamps removed, the screen will be tight.

When the screen is bent, staple or tack the screening at the other end and then remove the C-clamps. As the screen returns to its original flat shape, it will be stretched tight. Now, you will have to tack or staple the sides in place. Pull the screen material tight, and work from the center to the ends as you do the tacking. If there is a center rail on the screen, this should be the last to be tacked down.

When all of the screening has been tacked down, trim off the excess with a sharp knife and replace the molding. Be sure to sink the brads that hold the molding and fill the holes with putty. Paint over the putty and the job is done.

How to Replace Screen in Aluminum Frames

Screening is held in place on aluminum frames by pressure from a plastic strip. To remove the damaged screen, pull

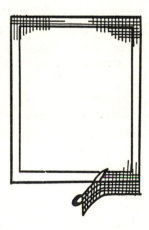

7-12-A
Trim the screening to the outside dimension of the frame.

out the plastic strip and you will be able to lift out the old screen.

Cut the new screen to the outside dimension of the frame; there will be excess, but it is needed to secure the screen. Position the new screening material over the opening and align it with all four sides of the frame. Begin on one of the long sides by pushing the plastic strip and the new screen

7-12-B
Use a tool, such as a screwdriver, to bend the screen
into the groove.

material into the groove on the frame. You can use a screw-driver blade to do this job. When one long side has been fastened, do the same on the other long side. Pull the screen-

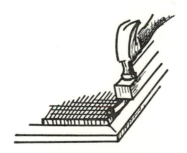

7-12-C
Use a hammer and a block to drive the plastic spline
into the groove.

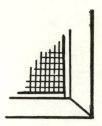

7-12-D
Use a butt joint where sections of spline meet at corners.

ing material tight to do this, but the action of the plastic strip being forced in the groove will add the final pressure needed to give you a nice, tight screen. When both long sides have been securely positioned, repeat the steps with both short sides.

If the plastic strip is soft, it can be damaged by the screwdriver blade. Try using a wood block and a light hammer. Place the block over the strip and tap it with a hammer. Move the block along as each section is set in the groove.

After the screen is in place, trim any excess screen that may show.

HOW TO FIX
DOORS AND LOCKS

A door is a barrier; it can seal out hot and cold weather, protect you from intruders and keep the smells from your workshop from invading the rest of the house. There are many kinds of doors, but they all open and close and are all subject to many of the same problems. Even though a door may have been hung perfectly, as a house settles, the door can begin to stick. Frequent use can also cause problems. However, door repairs are relatively easy to do, and it is better to get at the problems early before they become serious.

A door can also serve as an indicator of some other problems that may be taking place within your home. If you find a sticking door getting progressively worse, and the hinges are tight, it could mean that you are having some settling problems. Every house settles a little, but excessive tightening of a door in a relatively short period of time could be a warning. If the hinges are tight, it would be wise to have a carpenter look over the situation.

Before you take what appears to be an obvious step to correct a problem with a door, make sure that you know the real cause. For example, a door that binds against one section of the jamb invites a little planing or sanding at the binding point. This may work, but, because the problem can have several causes, it is best to diagnose it carefully before any wood is planed. If a hinge is loose, for example, this problem would occur, and the solution is often as simple as tightening the screws. But, if the hinges are tight and the wood has expanded, sanding and planing will be required.

Before you get into the diagnosis and solution of door problems, there are three basic repairs you should be familiar with that will help you work.

HOW TO REPAIR A WORN SCREW HOLE

If hinge screws are overtightened, the metal threads can ruin the grooves they had cut in the wood. The screws will no longer hold and the hinge will be loose. This problem can also occur when wood is very dry. Tightening and the weight of the door on the hinges can pull them free.

There are several ways to solve this problem. If it is a light, inside door, you can force some toothpicks or matchsticks which have been dipped into glue into the worn hole. After the glue has dried, drive a screw into the hole and the repair will have been completed. However, it is best to use a

8-1

Drive glue coated pegs into enlarged screw holes. After the glue dries, fresh pilot holes can be drilled that will hold the screws again.

screw that is slightly longer than the original screw to get a bite on fresh wood of the door.

For a stronger repair, or to solve the problem with a heavier door, shape a wooden dowel to the same configuration as the wood screw. Cut it a little longer than the screw. Cover this plug with wood glue and drive it into the stripped hole. When the glue has dried, trim off any excess peg that protrudes from the jamb. The screws can then be driven into the dowel plugs and the hinges will hang firmly.

HOW TO SHIM A HINGE

In some of the repairs to be described, the hinges will have to be pushed out a little from the jamb on which they have been mounted. To do this, you will have to add shims—spacers—between the back of the hinge and the jamb.

Shims can be made from a variety of materials, but because you will probably need to have some flexibility in the amount of shimming material you add in order to correct a problem, I suggest that you buy some thin brass shim stock. If necessary, you can stack two pieces of shim material to position the door correctly, but if you start with a heavy material, the thickness may be too much.

However, if this shim stock is not available, you can make the spacers from anything that will not compress easily. Actually, some of the cardboard used to make office file folders will work well, as will the metal from a discarded tin can.

To make the shim, place the surface of the hinge that contacts the jamb on the shim material and trace it with a pencil. Mark the centers of the screw holes very carefully. Don't cut the shim to include the part of the hinge that connects the second half; the shim should cover only the flat area in contact with the jamb.

Cut the shim about $1/32$ of an inch smaller than the dimension of the hinge. If you are cutting from cardboard, you can use a knife and a straight edge or a pair of scissors. Metal shims are most easily cut with a pair of tin snips.

Drill the holes and make sure that they match the holes in the hinge. After you have checked the hole alignment and made sure that none of the shim edges protrude from the hinge, you can mount the hinge over the shim. Don't glue the shim to the hinge or the jamb. You may want to remove them at a later date and this could present a problem.

8-2
A cardboard shim behind a hinge will compensate
for an ill-fitting door.

HOW TO DEEPEN A HINGE MORTISE

If the mortise for the hinge has not been cut deeply enough, it is possible for the door to bind on the latch side. To solve this problem, you will have to remove the hinges and deepen the mortises. You can determine if this is a problem by checking to see if the exposed surface of the hinge is flush with the wood on which it is mounted.

Deepening a mortise should be done very carefully. If you cut away too much wood you will be faced with the problem of shimming out the door.

To deepen a mortise, use a sharp wood chisel and a hammer. The chisel blade should be placed almost flat with respect to the surface of the mortise. This way, you will not run the risk of cutting too deeply by accident.

Holding the chisel firmly, tap the handle lightly with the hammer and work the blade from side to side. Try to trim away the wood in paper-thin strips as you go. It will be like planing with the plane blade just barely extended. After you have removed a thick, even, layer of wood, try the hinge in place. If more material must be removed, use the chisel to cut another thin layer. This is strictly a "cut-and-try" task that must be continued in this fashion until the hinge is flat.

HOW TO REMOVE A DOOR

Many of the repairs will require that a door be removed first. You can save yourself some trouble if you follow these steps when you do the job. First of all, open the door enough so that you will be able to work on the hinges. Then, slide something under the door to support it while the hinges are being removed. This could be a door wedge, a few magazines, or some heavy cardboard. When the door has been properly supported, remove the pin from the bottom hinge first. With a hammer and block of wood, or a screwdriver, tap up against the head of the pin. Unless it is stuck under many layers of paint, it should be fairly easy to remove, but seldom are these pins hand-tight. After the lower pin has been removed, tap out the upper hinge pin. The door will be untethered at this point, so be careful that it isn't knocked over. It helps to have someone hold the door while the pins are being removed. No strength is required; it's just a matter of keeping the door upright.

After both pins have been removed, pull the door away from the jamb hinges and you will be ready for any repairs that are required.

When you replace the hinges, wipe the pins with a light coat of oil before you drive them in place. Replace the top hinge first and then the bottom. Don't drive the pins all the way in until both hinges are aligned correctly.

HOW TO FIX A STICKING DOOR

Doors stick in different places, but when you know where the binding is taking place, you will have a pretty good idea of what must be done to solve the problem. In addition to the steps just outlined, the only other work that may be required is some sanding or light planing. Let's look at all the ways that a door can stick and what you can do to fix it.

1. When a door sticks at the top of the latch side and at the bottom of the saddle or floor, the first place to check is the top hinge. If the hinge is loose, tighten

8-3
When a door binds at the top, it can often be cured
by tightening the upper hinge or shimming
out the lower.

the screws. If the screws no longer bite into the wood, fill the holes as described, and drive the screws again. It is also possible that, when the door was hung, the mortise for the upper hinge was not cut deep enough.

Check to see if the hinge is flush with the jamb. If it isn't, deepen the mortise so the hinge fits properly.

If these steps fail, try shimming out the bottom hinge. This step will lift the bottom of the door and tend to angle the door away from the top part of the jamb where it is sticking.

Of course, it is possible that the jamb is badly out of shape from settling. If this is the case, be sure to have a professional determine the cause.

2. If your door sticks up against the head jamb and binds against the lower portion of the jamb on the latch side, check the top hinge first. It may be necessary to shim this hinge a little. If this fails, or only relieves the binding partially, see if the lower hinge is loose. If

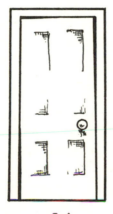

8-4
When a door binds at the bottom on the latch side,
it can often be fixed by tightening the lower hinge,
or by shimming out the upper.

tightening the lower hinge fails to solve the problem, see if the lower hinge is mounted properly. It may be necessary to deepen the mortise. Do this in very small steps, checking the spots where the door sticks regularly.

3. If the binding occurs only on the hinge side of the door, the chances are good that you can solve it with some shims. If the binding takes place along the entire length of the door where it meets the jamb, shim both hinges equally until the problem has been solved. If the problem seems to be located near only one of the hinges, apply the shims to that hinge until the problem has been solved.

   During this repair, you may push the door far enough so that it will bind against the jamb on the latch side. If this happens, sand away enough wood on the door to solve the binding. However, you will probably not have to do much sanding, so take it easy and don't make a big gap on this side.

   If the latch side binds badly, it's best to solve the problem by working on the hinge side. To plane the entire latch side, the lock must be removed and it will require careful refinishing. The hinge side is seldom visible and refinishing is less critical. See the next step.

4. When a door binds badly on both sides, you will have to remove the door and plane it on the hinge side only. When the door has been planed enough to fit properly, you will probably have to deepen the hinge mortises to make the fit.

5. When it is apparent that a door is sticking because the wood has swollen, and it is not the fault of the hinges, you can sand or plane the spots that bind. But bear in mind that such swelling will disappear as the weather changes. If you plane away too much wood, you may leave a noticeable gap.

Keep These Things in Mind

Whenever you have problems with a sticking door, try to keep the hinge side parallel with the jamb. If the door was hung properly, and the jamb is square, the door should work when the hinge problems are solved.

You should resist using a plane right away. A plane can take away quite a bit of wood before you realize it. Start with coarse sandpaper, or a belt sander, and follow up with a fine paper.

Be sure to make marks on the area that is to be planed, otherwise you may cut into areas that already fit well.

When planing across the grain of the end of a side rail, move the plane from the outside edge toward the center to avoid splintering. You can plane over the edge when you are working in the direction of the grain.

HOW TO FIX A DOOR THAT WILL NOT LATCH

When a door warps, or the house settles, there can be some misalignment of the door and the frame. At the least, it may take a bit of a slam to get the door to latch. At worst it becomes impossible for the latch to engage the strike plate at all. Let's look at the simplest problem and solution first.

If, because of a slight warp or some settling, the bolt is slightly out of alignment with the hole in the latch plate, it is often possible solve the problem with a little filing. Close the door and place a piece of carbon paper between the bolt and the strike plate. Close the bolt against the carbon paper, and then open it. Note the place on the strike plate where the bolt has left a mark. If it is only a small area, you can file the opening a little to accommodate the bolt.

If the door is not warped, but the strike plate and bolt are sufficiently out of alignment to make the filing step impractical, you will have to realign the plate. Remove the strike plate and use the bolt and carbon paper to indicate on the door jamb where the bolt should engage. Use a chisel to alter the mortise. Then, re-mount the strike plate in the new position. In most cases, this repositioning will be only a short distance from the old location.

There are times when all of the wood in the door and frame will shrink enough so that the latch bolt will just not reach the strike plate. When this happens, try adding shims

8-5
When a latch bolt fails to contact the strike plate,
the problem can often be solved by shimming out
the strike plate.

under the strike plate until the bolt enters the hole in the strike plate. In extreme cases, it may also be necessary to add shims under the hinges to position the door closer to the latch plate.

If there is a warp near the top or the bottom of the door and it is difficult to secure the latch, you might try using partial shims under the hinges. The job of the shim is to change the mounting angle of the door to compensate for the warp. The partial shims should be placed under the hinge leaves on the pin side only, and they can be used on the door or the jamb side. Often, this minor correction will be enough to make the latch work.

However, you may find it necessary to reposition the stop to make the door close. Before you remove the old stop, use a sharp knife or razor blade to score the paint along the joint of the stop and the jamb. This will prevent the paint from chipping and cracking when the stop is being removed.

After the paint has been scored, pry the stop away from the jamb gently with a wide paint scraper. Remove, but save the nails.

Next, close and latch the door. With the door latched, place the stop in position on the jamb and the door and draw a light line to indicate the new position. To accommodate all the variations possible, it is a good idea to place a piece of thin cardboard between the door and the stop before the line is drawn. This will allow for enough change in the wood to make sure the job won't have to be done again in the near future.

Leave the door closed and the shim in place before you renail the stop in place. Press the stop tightly against the cardboard shim and renail the stop in place. It's best to just tack the stop in place before you drive the nails in fully to make sure that the repair will work. Once you are sure that the door will latch, you can set the nails.

HOW TO CORRECT A WARPED DOOR

Doors warp for a number of reasons, but most of the problems are caused by weather. As seasons change and humidity comes and goes, wood expands and contracts. In all but the most seasoned woods there will be some warping. Here's how to handle the problem.

If a door is warped on the hinge side and somewhere in the middle between the top and bottom, the problem can often be corrected by mounting a third hinge between the two existing hinges. The hinge will have to be mounted in a mortise, just as the two original hinges are, and the job often solves the problem.

To cure a larger warp, more drastic measures are often required. Try removing the door and placing it on supports outside in the sun. The supports should be placed at either end and should support the width of the door at each end. The warped side should be positioned so that it faces up. Next, wet the door, and place some heavy weights over the bulge.

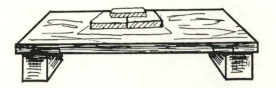

8-6
A warped door can often be straightened by placing weights
over the bulging section. Position the door bulge side up.

Leave the door out in the sun to dry for at least two days. The
surface of the door should be protected from damage from the
weights by paper, cloth, or some other material.

When the door has been dried by the sun, remove the
weights and see if it fits. More often than not, this will have
done the job, but, if only a small warp is left and you have
latch problems, it's best to try to solve the latch problems
another way rather than to continue to try to straighten the
door more. You have little control over the process and the
warp may just go the other way.

Warped doors can also be corrected by using a
turnbuckle and wire arrangement. This can be done while the
door is being used. Locate the highest point in the bulge and
mark it. From this point, draw a line to the closest jamb-side
corner. With these two points, extend the line to the other
side. Mount heavy screw eyes at each end of the line. Place a
2 × 4 block (long-side out) right over the bulge. Connect the
two screw eyes with wire and a turnbuckle. Tighten the
turnbuckle until there is pressure on the wire. As the bulge
flattens, take up turns until the door has flattened completely. You can now remove the screw eyes, wire and turnbuckle.
Of course, if this door has been decorated, fill the holes made
by the screw eyes, and paint over the filler.

This repair should be made gradually. Take up only half a
turn every few days. And, when the warp has been fixed,
leave the brace on for a week or so longer before you remove
it.

HOW TO REPLACE A SADDLE

The saddle, or threshhold, takes a lot of abuse; just plain wear from the foot traffic plus rain, if it is part of an outside door, all contribute to the damage. However, saddles are usually made of long-wearing oak, and they will last a long time.

If you have to replace the door saddle, try to remove it in one piece so that it can be used as a pattern. Check the door construction carefully before you begin pulling up the threshold. If it extends under the jambs, you may have to remove the stop molding to do the job. If it appears that nothing short of disassembling the door frame will do the job, an easy solution to the problem is to saw the saddle into three separate parts. Make the first two cuts with a back saw near both jambs so that you can lift out the center section. With

8-7-A
A saddle can be removed by cutting it in two places.
Remove the center section first, and then pry out
the two side sections.

this portion free, it is a simple matter to slide the two end sections from under the jamb.

Even if you had to resort to sawing the saddle apart, it can still be used as a pattern. But, you will have to compensate for the thickness of the saw blade when you assemble the pieces to make the tracing. Just lay the three parts in their proper relationship to each other on a piece of paper, but position them by inserting the saw blade between them. When you make the tracing, be sure that the pieces don't move.

Use the pattern to outline the shape on a new piece of oak saddle. Make the cutouts, and make a trial fit between the door jambs. If it is tight, don't force it; you can upset the

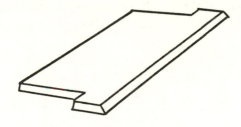

8-7-B
Cut the new saddle to the same dimensions
as the old saddle.

frame and ruin the alignment of the door. Just cut a little at a time at the points which appear to bind. The saddle should fit snugly, but not tightly.

When you are sure that the saddle fits perfectly, position it and drill pilot holes for the nails. It isn't advisable to drive nails through oak—it can split, and you can bend a lot of nails before you get one through. Oak is a tough wood. Use 2½" finishing nails to secure the saddle in position. Countersink the nails, fill the holes with wood putty and stain and finish the wood to match the rest of the trim.

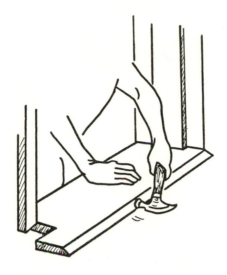

8-7-C
Tap the new saddle in place. Drill pilot holes and nail the
new saddle in place. Saddles are usually made of oak,
and pilot holes will be necessary.

HOW TO INSTALL A PEEPHOLE

If you have an outside door with no windows, you might want to be able to see who is on the other side before you open it. You can install a peephole for this purpose, and there are several types to consider. One is simply a small metal frame with a metal latch over it. When using this, the person on the outside will be aware that you are looking out.

There is another device which is essentially a wide-angle lens. This arrangement allows you to look out and get a good view of the person without being observed yourself.

Whichever type of peephole you select, the mounting instructions are similar. A hole of the right size to accommodate the device must be cut in the door. This hole can be cut with a keyhole saw or with a drill of the appropriate size. If you use a

8-8
Use a keyhole saw to cut a hole for a peephole. Cut the hole
to accommodate the peephole system you have bought.

keyhole saw, you will have to cut a pilot hole with a smaller
drill in order to start the saw cut.

Doors vary in thickness, and the different types of
peepholes are designed to accommodate this variation. Follow the instructions packed with the peephole you buy to
insure proper mounting.

HOW TO INSTALL WEATHERSTRIPPING

Weatherstripping will help to reduce fuel bills by stopping heat leaks during the winter, and it can help your air
conditioner run more efficiently during the summer.

Weatherstripping is installed on outside doors in new
houses, but when it hasn't been positioned, or when the house
settles, some pretty big air leaks can develop. There are a
number of ways to weatherstrip a door, and each has its advantages and disadvantages. Some fairly sophisticated tech-
niques are used, but these methods require special tools and
training to install properly. If you want to have a professional
do the job, think about using J-strips—a system of interlock-
ing strips that are installed in rabbets in the door and frame
with special tools. Most experts agree that this system is
about the most efficient way to weatherstrip a door. It may be

more expensive than some other methods, but over the years the savings in fuel use will probably pay for the installation.

If your air leakage problem is minor, you can probably solve it in minutes and at the least expense with one of the adhesive backed foam weatherstripping materials. This self-

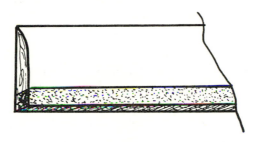

8-9
A wood strip with a foam backing is commonly used as
a door insulator.

sticking material is positioned to the inside face of the door stop. When the door is closed against it, the material compresses and seals the air leaks.

Rigid weatherstripping can be added to an outside door easily. This material is made of either aluminum or wood, and includes a soft facing material that contracts and seals when the door is closed. The wood stripping usually has a facing of foam, and it is installed by nailing it to the stop. The strip should be positioned on the stop and snugged up to the surface of the closed door before they are nailed up. Position the nails about 10″ apart, countersink them and fill the holes with wood putty. Paint or stain this wood weatherstripping to match the surface of the door.

The same principle has been applied to the manufacture of aluminum weatherstripping. The aluminum channel holds a piece of compressible plastic which, when positioned on the stop, will seal out the weather as the door is closed. This material must be cut to size with a hacksaw. It is installed with screws rather than nails. And, this type of stripping is often supplied with slots, rather than holes for mounting. The slots will allow you to adjust the pressure of the weather-stripping as changes take place in the door. This feature makes it easy to keep a house secure against the weather as settling takes place.

Several styles of spring metal weatherstripping are on the market and, when properly installed, they provide an excellent barrier. In general, this weatherstripping is supplied in two basic forms: a V-shaped strip or as a piece of crimped stock. Both types are installed by tacking the stripping to the frame, but because each manufacturer has his own variations of the design, it is best to follow the specific instructions packed with each set. It is best to begin the job on the hinge side and to only tack the strip in place before any final nailing is done. With the strip lightly tacked, test the door for closure. If it doesn't close, find the binding spot and sand it down. It is important to note that the spring leaf weatherstripping should be applied so that the fold of the metal is in the direction of the closing door. If the stripping is applied in the other direction, as the door is closed it will ruin the stripping.

If the entire door frame is to be protected with spring metal weatherstripping, be sure to miter the corners where the sides and the top meet. If you fail to do this, pressure from the door will ruin the stripping.

Threshold weatherstripping is made in two basic styles: a sweep system which mounts on the bottom of the door and a gasket type which is attached directly to the threshold or the door. Both work well, but if you have a high carpet inside the room served by the door, you may have problems with the sweep type as the door is opened and closed. The bottom of the sweep can rub on the carpet and wear it down.

The gasket type of threshold insulation can be mounted on an existing threshold, or, there are models that can be bought that come equipped with a replacement threshold of

8-10-A
An aluminum frame holds a vinyl seal in position to provide
effective insulation of the bottom of a door.

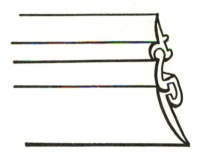

8-10-B
Flap-type weatherstripping springs out of the way
when the door is opened. The upper section is rigid
and mounted to the door.

metal. These systems all require a certain amount of clearance between the bottom of the door and the threshold—usually about ½". To insure that you have the right amount of space, first measure the distance from the top of the saddle to the bottom of the door. If the gap is not wide enough, make a mark on the bottom of the door to make sure that you plane enough and not too much off the bottom. Remove the door and do the planing. Be sure to plane from the hinge and latch sides to the middle to avoid splintering the wood. Follow the line and make sure that you leave the bottom planed evenly and smoothly.

Some gasket types of weatherstripping include a boot, or metal channel that is mounted on the bottom of the door. This boot has a taper to make it easier to close the door and to insure a snug, weather-tight seal. Be sure that it is installed so that the higher side is the first to contact the gasket as the door is closed.

Both the gasket base and the shoe will usually have to be cut to the size of the door. This can be done with a hacksaw, but it's best to remove the gasket (it will slide out of the frame) and cut it separately with a sharp knife. A hacksaw blade can shred the plastic material if it is cut along with the aluminum.

When all of the trimming has been done, and the gasket carrier and shoe installed, re-hang the door. Check the closure carefully. The seal should be made with the plastic in the carrier and the shoe on the door. There should be no metal to metal or metal to wood contact between the strip that holds the gasket and the door. If there is such contact, remove the door and plane away enough wood to make the proper seal. If you don't, the gasket will wear out very quickly.

I have only hit on some of the more common types of weatherstripping. There are a number of other practical systems on the market and most of them work very well. Because each system is mounted somewhat differently than the others, it is impossible to give specific instructions in this chapter. However, if you follow the principles I have outlined and the instructions packed with the weatherstripping you have bought, you should have little or no trouble with your installation.

HOW TO FIX SLIDING DOORS

Sliding doors are most often made of wood or glass and they all must be supported top and bottom in guides or tracks.

Some sliding doors are hung from the top and others slide on bottom rails. Usually, light closet doors and very heavy garage doors are supported from the top; medium weight doors, such as those which serve a patio, are bottom-supported.

Perhaps the most common problem occurs with sliding doors that are supported from the bottom. When dirt accumulates or foreign objects fall into the tracks, the door may, at first, be difficult to move. But, if the problem is not cleared up, it is possible to jam a sliding door. If cleaning the section of track that is visible doesn't do the job, you will have to remove the door and clean the track thoroughly. In most cases, removal is just a matter of lifting the door enough to clear the bottom track, angling it slightly away from the track and lifting it free of the upper track. Even if you are working with a light closet door, the job should be done by two people. It's just an awkward job, and no matter where you put your hands to lift the door free of the track, you probably will be in a bad position for leverage when you are ready to swing the door out. Play it safe; have a friend help.

If the door is hung from top rails, you may have a little more trouble removing it. Top-hung doors are supported on sets of casters that ride within the tracks mounted above the door. To prevent these doors from accidentally jumping the track during rough handling, they are often held in place by a locking track. The tracks on some top-mounted doors are notched so that the caster wheels can be lifted free only in one position. If the track is recessed so that you can't spot the notches, you will just have to experiment an inch or two at a time by lifting and tilting the door. When you reach the notch, the door will tilt further and you will be able to lift it free of the track. When you discover the notch, make a little mark on the threshold of the position of the door. This will make it easier to reinstall the door and to remove it in the future, if it becomes necessary.

Some top track mounted sliding doors are spring loaded. That is, a little upward pressure beyond that required to just lift the door will free it from the track.

When you have the door removed, inspect every inch of the track for accumulated debris and for objects that can block the operation or force the door off its track.

Apart from some light and simple sliding doors, most of these closures are supported and moved by a set of adjustable roller wheels. If your door is hanging unevenly, the chances are good that one of the wheel assemblies might have slipped. Because there are so many different types of support wheel systems on the market, it is impossible to give instructions for the adjustment of all of them. But all work on the same general principle; the position of the wheel, as it relates to the door and the track can be adjusted enough to compensate for settling and other variations. Many of the support wheel systems use some form of an inclined plane to facilitate the adjustments. That is, the wheels are screw-mounted to the door, but the screw holes are not round—they are elongated and positioned at an angle relative to the top of the door. As the wheel is slid back and forth slightly on the loosened mounting screws, it will move closer or further away from the rails. It's an easy system to adjust, but to do it right, be sure to support the top-hung door from below by something which is as thick as the clearance you want. And, be sure that the door is supported evenly before the adjusting screws are tightened. A long strip of heavy cardboard or wood shims can be used to hold the door in position, but be sure to remove them before you put the door into regular operation.

The mounting wheels are usually made of nylon, so no lubrication is needed with most sliding doors.

HOW TO FIX LOCK PROBLEMS

There are a number of different types of locks, and latching mechanisms are made for doors which lead out of the house as well as doors which connect interior rooms. The locks which are used to latch doors between rooms are usually tubular locks and they do not have any key-locking cylinder.

However, some can be locked by pressing a latch or a button in the center of the knob on the other side through which you can insert a nail to open the door in an emergency. It's just a matter of pressing the point of the nail on a release trap inside the lock.

All locks have some problems in common. Let's take a look at some of these problems and how you can solve them.

How to Fix a Sticky Lock

When a lock becomes difficult to turn, the chances are good that it has become gummed up. If the lock has been oiled, dust has probably collected in the mechanism to make the whole lock a sticky mess.

Remove the lock (see the instructions in this chapter for each lock). Disassemble the lock, but make absolutely sure that you know how it is to be reassembled. Next, clean all of the parts in a solvent, such as paint thinner. Be sure to ventilate the room when you use the solvent. When the lock is clean and the solvent has dried, reassemble the lock and lubricate it with powdered graphite, silicone spray, light oil, or light grease. *However, you should never lubricate the cylinder with anything but powdered graphite.* The tumbler pins and the keyway should be lubricated by blowing the powdered graphite into the keyhole. You can also apply graphite to the key and slide it in and out until the graphite finds its way to the pins and the surface of the tumbler. Don't overlubricate the other parts of the lock with whatever lubrication you choose to use.

If you do not have any powdered graphite, you can make some by rubbing an ordinary lead pencil across the teeth of a file. Don't use sandpaper; the grit from the paper will mix with the graphite and cause more problems than the application of the powder will solve.

Somehow, all of us adapt to changing conditions, and I once heard of a man who had a front door lock that had slowly gotten so sticky that he could no longer use it. The latch worked, so he could secure the door. Over a few months, he had become so accustomed to not locking his door that he forgot about repairing the lock. You guessed it—a burglar discovered his lazy habit and cleaned him out. For a few cents worth of graphite, and fifteen minutes of time, he could have prevented a $10,000 loss.

How to Remove a Broken Key

When a key breaks in a lock, it usually breaks flush with the surface. When this happens, it is often possible to use a bent pin pushed in over the top of the lock to pull the broken section out just enough to get a grip on it with pliers. If the key is in too tightly, try drilling a tiny hole on the thickest portion of the exposed end of the broken key. The hole need not be deep; an eighth of an inch is usually sufficient. Next,

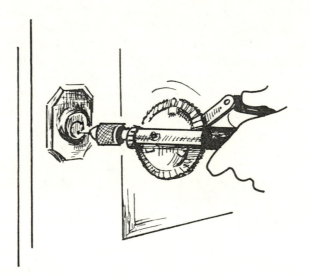

8-11
Drill a small hole in the end of the broken key.
The tip of a fine screw can be fitted in the hole
and used to withdraw the key.

use a small, fine-thread wood or sheet metal screw to tap into the hole. It's only necessary to get enough of a grip with the threads so that a little of the key can be pulled from the keyway. When enough of the key has been exposed, use pliers to remove it.

If this doesn't work and you can remove the lock, you will be able to push the broken key out from the other side of the disassembled lock.

How to Fix a Jammed Key

A key can jam in a lock for several reasons. If the lock is all gunked up with gritty oil, the key can stick. And, if the key was positioned incorrectly and forced in, it will probably stick. In either case, use a little powdered graphite and work the key free gradually. Don't try to work the key loose by banging it; you may do more harm than good.

If, after you have removed the key, it turns out that the problem was the result of a gummy lock, take the lock apart, clean it, lubricate it and reassemble it in the door.

How to Unfreeze a Lock

It isn't necessary for water to enter a lock for it to freeze in the cold weather; moist air is often enough to create the problem when the temperature drops below freezing.

The solution is easy and requires a pair of pliers, and some matches or a lighter. Hold the key by the handle with the pliers and warm it with the lighter. Don't make it red hot, but it should be quite warm. Push the warmed key into the keyway; if it only goes a little way, leave it where it is and use the lighter to warm the key some more. Push it in a little further. Even when you have the key all the way in, the tumbler may still be frozen. Just continue heating the key handle until the lock turns freely. Be careful not to force the key; you could break it off in the lock and have another problem on your hands.

How to Fix a Stuck Bolt

When the latch bolt will not engage or disengage without a little jiggling of the door, you should look at the hinges first. If they are loose and out of alignment, the bolt will not be able to seat in the strike plate in the jamb. Tighten the hinges before you try anything else. It may be necessary to shim one of the hinges to bring the bolt into alignment with the hole in the strike plate.

If the bolt is sticking within the lock, and not in the strike plate, look for collected paint on the surface and inspect the lock to make sure that it is not seized up with dirty lubrication.

How to Fix a Latchbolt That No Longer Engages the Strike Plate

If the door has warped, or the house has settled, the length of the latchbolt may no longer reach and hold with the strike plate. The first thing to try is a shim under the strike plate. A piece of heavy cardboard will often do the job. Or, you can mount a second strike plate right over the first. To do this, remove the screws on the original and position an identical plate over the first. Use the screws to hold both plates in place.

What to Do When a Second Key Fails to Work

There is usually more than one key for each house lock. But one key is usually used more often. When this happens, the key and the lock wear evenly and will continue to open the door easily. But, when the seldom-used key is tried, there may be enough wear so that it will not engage the tumblers. The solution is to have a duplicate made from the most often-used key.

How to Remove a Cylinder or Tubular Lock

Most cylinder and tubular locks are installed the same way. You must begin removal of these locks from the inside.

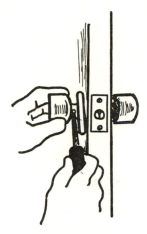

8-12-A
Push the button on the shank and the knob will be freed.

8-12-B
Pry off the cover plate, and then remove the two screws that
hold the lock in place.

There is usually a button or catch on the handle shank inside
that, when pushed, allows you to remove the inner handle.

8-12-C
Remove the assembly.

When the handle has been removed, there may be an escutcheon covering a retaining plate, or you may be able to remove
the screws directly. If the screw heads are covered by an
escutcheon, it will snap off to expose the screws that hold the
lock assembly in the door. Remove the screws and slip the

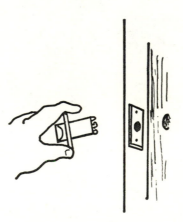

8-12-D
Remove the latch assembly.

lock out of the door. When you remove the screws that are in the bolt plate, the latch assembly can be removed.

To replace the lock, just reverse the instructions.

How to Remove a Mortise Lock

Mortise locks are installed in recesses cut in the door, and in general, there are two types of locks. One is used on inside doors and seldom contains a dead bolt. This lock usually consists only of a knob-operated latch.

Mortise locks used on outside doors usually include a dead bolt so that the door can be locked. Usually, a key operates the dead bolt from the outside, but the lock is operated from the inside by a small knob. Some exterior mortise locks are activated from the outside by a thumb lever and others use knobs on both sides. In any case, despite all the varia-

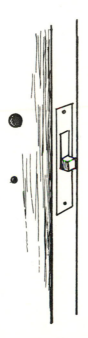

8-13-A
Remove knob, and pull shaft free.

tions, there is enough in common so that all mortise locks can be removed in much the same way.

Begin by removing the knobs from both sides of the lock. A set screw at the base of the knob usually holds the knob in place. Pull the connecting shaft free. Remove the screws from the face of the lock on the door edge and you will be able to slide out the old mortise lock mechanism.

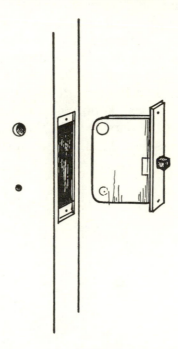

8-13-B
Remove the screws holding the lock in place.

Some mortise locks are a bit more complicated because they often include cylinder locks to secure a dead bolt. There are a number of different systems, but if you work from the inside, you should be able to determine just how the lock was installed in order to disassemble it properly.

Apart from cleaning or making simple repairs, most mortise locks are removed in order to install new and safer locks.

There are a number of different types of locks that can be installed where an old mortise lock seems inadequate. Because of the variety of styles, it is just about impossible to give specific instructions for installation. However, such installations usually require that a new hole be drilled to accommodate the operating mechanism. Often, it is possible to borrow or rent a drill of sufficient size to do the job, rather than to invest in the tool for a very limited use.

Each replacement lock is packed with very specific instructions, including templates for accurate drilling. If you follow the instructions packed with the replacement lock that you buy, the chances are good that you will be able to install the new lock without a hitch.

HOW TO SOLVE GARAGE DOOR PROBLEMS

Garage doors either swing in and out, or they swing up inside the garage on a set of tracks. Most of the newer houses have garage doors that swing up, and there are two basic types of overhead doors. One system uses a solid door which swings out quite a bit as it moves up into its overhead track. The other type of garage door is made in hinged sections, and folds as it moves upwards.

Overhead doors are made with counterbalancing systems. Heavy springs offset the weight so that it takes very little effort to lift or lower these doors.

Most problems with overhead garage doors are a result of either poor maintenance, or the great unsupported center weight of the door as it is held in position in its tracks.

How to Fix Overhead Garage Door Track Problems

A lot of pressure is exerted on the tracks that hold overhead doors. Combine this with wood that dries out and you can have problems with overhead door tracks.

If the tracks are loose, or appear to be uneven, go over

every bolt and screw that has been used to secure the tracks. Tighten them all, and if you find any holes that have worn to the point where the screws no longer hold, fill the hole with a glued dowel before you attempt to re-drive the bolt. However, if you find more than one such problem don't—under any circumstances—remove more than one bolt at a time to fill the holes. The entire door system could tumble down on you with serious consequences.

A lot of careless activity takes place in a garage; snow shovels are tossed aside when the season is over and lawn mowers are pushed aside to make room for bicycles and other things. During any of this, a heavy object could bump a track and bend it out of shape, or dent in one of the sides. When this happens, you will have trouble operating the door. Such dents and bends can often be fixed with a heavy pair of pliers or with a long-handled wrench. However, as you bend or pry, do it gradually and keep an eye on other parts of the track that are holding the door. If you bend too much or too quickly, you just might bring the door down on you.

If you have spring problems, it is often best to have a professional take a look. Some springs are under considerable pressure, and, if broken, could hurt you badly.

When the latch bolts on the sides of an overhead door fail to engage the strike plate, it is usually because of settling or wear in all parts of the door. The strike plates are usually supplied with mounting slots, rather than holes. To reset the plates, just loosen the screws and position the plates so they will accept the bolt when it is thrown.

Tracks that have become twisted will often bind as the roller wheel is operated. Follow each of the roller wheels through one complete open and closing cycle and re-shape the track wherever binding occurs.

How to Prevent Rot and Air Leaks

The bottom of an overhead door usually has gaps between itself and the floor of the garage. To solve this problem, it is a simple matter to nail on a form of weatherstripping that compresses well as the door is closed. But, before you add the weatherstripping, be sure to paint the bottom of the door with a good wood preservative.

HOW TO FIX STEPS, WALKS, WALLS AND DRIVEWAYS

Most people think that brick and masonry will last forever and never need any maintenance; not true! For example, crumbling mortar in a brick wall may just look unsightly to you, but it can be a source of serious moisture problems within the house. A crack in a foundation may be easy to fill, but it is often the sign of far more serious trouble. The point is this: treat masonry with the same attention as you would any other material used to build a house.

Brick steps are very pretty and practical, but like most other masonry materials, they can be damaged by weather. In one case I was told of, ice had loosened one brick at the top of a set of steps leading to the front door of a house. The owner put off replacing the brick and merely left it loosely in its socket. The brick was not in the middle of a step, and the owner reasoned that no one would step on it until he got around to making the repair. But, as bad luck would have it, several friends were climbing the steps at one time, and one person, off to the side, did step on the loose brick. Without going into the details, the person was hurt badly in the fall that followed. The homeowner was covered by liability insurance, but his put-it-off attitude had seriously injured a friend. Even though the friend forgave him, he always held himself responsible for the accident.

Before you undertake any of the repairs that require the use of mortar, read the next few paragraphs. When you understand what mortar is and how it should be used, you will be much better able to do the work.

HOW TO MIX MORTAR

Mortar is a mixture of some type of binder and sand. Water is used to make a mixture that, when dry, will hold bricks in place; or, it can be used by itself as a structural material. The binder is a mixture of cement, lime or both materials. The sand must be specially prepared for use in masonry work. If it has any clay or organic matter in it, it will be weak. Be sure that you buy sand that is washed and prepared especially for making mortar. You can test the quality of the sand by rubbing a handful between both palms of your hands. After a minute or so, your hands should still be clean; there should be no stain. And never use sea sand; the salts in it will prevent you from getting a good joint and it will discolor. Be sure that the water you use is clean. Anything in the water, such as dust and dirt, will reduce the strength of the bond. Use only fresh water; salt water should never be used to make mortar.

There are a number of different types of mortar and each has its own advantages. But most of these mixes are used in new construction or for large scale repair work. For the repairs that are described in this chapter, it is best either to buy a pre-mixed material which contains not only the cement, but the sand as well. All you have to do is add an appropriate amount of water and you are ready to work. However, this is the most expensive way to do the job. But, because cement deteriorates with age, unless you plan to use a lot of it, the pre-mixed material may be the best bet after all. You could end up throwing away unused cement a year from now.

When you use the pre-mixed material, follow the instructions on the bag carefully. Add just the right amount of water and do the mixing in a very clean container. A well-scrubbed wheelbarrow or a clean bucket are most convenient.

Mix only enough mortar for an hour's use. Mortar will begin to set in this period, and working with it after an hour will result in a weakened joint. A professional can mix considerably more than an amateur because he has had experience with the material and can estimate how much time it will take to finish a job. It is best to mix less and do it more often if you are unfamiliar with the work.

If you want to mix your own mortar, the best, all-around mix can be made of one part masonry cement and three parts clean sand. Follow these general points and you should have a good mix:

1. Mix the dry ingredients thoroughly first.
2. Add the water a little at a time.
3. Mix until you get a mortar that slides easily from the trowel but can be piled on the trowel without sagging.

If you cannot locate masonry cement, you can make a good mortar with one part portland cement, one part hydrated lime and six parts sand.

HOW TO COLOR MORTAR

Some masonry structures are made with a coloring added to the mortar, and others that were made without coloring, may have darkened over the years. Whatever the case, you may want to color a repaired mortar joint.

Colors are available that can be added to mortar and you can mix up to 10 percent of the weight of the cement to do the job. Adding any larger amount of the dry coloring may weaken the mortar.

When coloring is used, it should be blended thoroughly with the dry ingredients before the water is added. Because the colors do change somewhat when they dry, it is best to make a few small samples and let them dry before making the final colored mortar. Be sure to record the amounts of color used so you can mix the same proportions when you are ready to do the repair. Check the color after the test mixes have dried. Colored mortar tends to dry somewhat lighter than it appears when wet.

HOW TO USE MORTAR

When mortar is used to repair an existing structure, the surface on which it is to be applied should be wet thoroughly. However, there should be no free water on the surface. If the surfaces dry during the repair, dampen them before more mortar is applied.

If you are holding the mortar on a piece of wood as you use it, the wood should be wet first or it will draw water from the mix and weaken it.

If this is the first time you are working with mortar, you may be a little slow and it may begin to set before you use all of your mixture. You can extend the usefulness of the mixture a little by adding some water. But do not add very much—it will definitely weaken the mixture.

The weather has a very pronounced effect on the working time of mixed mortar. On a hot, dry day, the mortar will harden much faster than in cool, damp weather.

HOW TO USE A TROWEL

For the repairs described in this chapter, you will be better off using a small pointing trowel, rather than the larger trowel used for masonry construction. The pointing trowel will be easier to handle and it is more adaptable to the small repairs described in this chapter.

It's often a good idea to practice a little before you undertake a job involving the use of mortar and a trowel. You can mix the mortar with a trowel and the trowel can be used to apply it as well as to handle the finishing strokes.

If you have your mixed mortar on a hawk, or another flat surface, practice cutting off just enough to cover the trowel, and drawing it away from the main pile. When this section has been separated, slip the trowel under it and lift it cleanly away.

The flat side of the trowel is used to smooth mortar in place, and the point and edge are used to trim away the ex-

9-1
The flat side of the trowel is used to force mortar
into the joints.

cess. The point is used to pack mortar between bricks when you are replacing damaged sections. The tip is also used for "pointing," which is described in the next section.

Using a trowel is more a matter of becoming accustomed to handling it in a way that is most comfortable, rather than trying to copy the skills of a master bricklayer. Practice a little, and when you are ready to handle a repair, the job should go smoothly.

HOW TO CURE CONCRETE

Most inexperienced amateur masons stop after they have filled a crack or poured a patch, thinking that all that remains is for the mortar to harden. Harden it will, but if it is not cared for properly during the hardening period, the new material will be weak and subject to cracking. Improperly dried concrete will almost always have a dusty service, no matter how often it is brushed.

The new mortar must be cured—prevented from drying too quickly. When the drying process is slowed down, the concrete will be stronger and more water-resistant. To say that all concrete must be left to cure for a specific period of time is impossible, because weather conditions vary all over the country. In a hot, dry climate, water evaporates more rapidly than it does in a cooler and damper region. However, if you want a rule of thumb, six or seven days of proper curing is usually adequate in any climate, as long as the concrete is kept damp.

Curing consists of keeping the fresh mortar moist as it hardens. After the new material has hardened, the best bet is to cover it with a piece of burlap and to keep the burlap wet with a moist spray from a garden hose.

If the concrete is not exposed to the sun or wind, a burlap covering may not be necessary; just give it a light spray often enough to keep it damp for a week.

HOW TO REPOINT BRICK

The joints between bricks in walls, chimneys and other surfaces can be damaged over the years by changes in the weather. When this happens, the entire structure can weaken, but the problem must be quite severe for this to happen. More often, however, the main problem is one of moisture penetration into the house. When this happens, it will be necessary to remove some of the mortar and to replace it with fresh. The finishing strokes are called pointing.

There are a number of different ways the joints between bricks are finished off. But, when you do this job, you will want to use the same pointing technique that was used on the wall originally. Most of the angular pointing strokes can be made with the trowel, but the round groove, often called a grapevine, must be made with some rounded tool that conforms to the shape of the original groove. A wood stick or dowel rounded to the right contour works perfectly.

Begin the job by removing the mortar between the bricks to about a ½″ depth. Do this with a chisel and a hammer, but be careful that you don't damage any of the bricks in the process. If you hold the chisel at a sharp angle and use light taps with the hammer, you will reduce the possibility of damaging the brick.

Important: Wear safety glasses or goggles when you do this or any masonry repair described in this chapter. Chips will fly every which way, and you can hurt your eyes if you are not careful.

If you have a lot of wall to repoint, it's best to work in smaller, manageable units, rather than to attack the entire project at once. About a square yard is comfortable for most people who don't make a living at this sort of thing.

Just about any small cold chisel can be used, but the easiest to use is a cape chisel. Work on the vertical joints first.

9-2
Use a hammer and chisel to remove old and
crumbling mortar.

When you have the mortar removed to the required depth, brush the wall and the joints vigorously; there should be no loose mortar or powder in the joints when the new mortar is applied.

Next, dampen the entire surface with a fine spray from a garden hose. Use sufficient water so the bricks absorb enough to prevent them from drawing water from the freshly applied mortar. There should be no free water on the surface, but it should be dampened thoroughly.

Mix the mortar, as described earlier in this chapter, and use the small pointing trowel to apply it to the vertical joints first. If you are coloring the mortar, make it slightly darker than the old mortar; it will dry somewhat lighter than it appears when it is wet.

Force the mortar into all of the joints with the tip of the trowel, doing the vertical joints first. Finish the joints with the tip of the trowel as you go along to conform to the style

9-3
Use a pointing trowel to make the same joints
as the original work.

used in the original construction. Try to avoid getting mortar on the exposed surfaces of the bricks as you work and clean up as you go. When the mortar hardens, brush off any excess.

You should keep the repaired area dampened for several days after the fresh mortar has been applied. If left to dry without dampening, the bricks will draw moisture from the mortar and leave you with weakened material. Use a fine spray from a garden hose or cover it with wet burlap.

HOW TO FIX LARGE CRACKS
CAUSED BY SETTLING

Every house has some settling problems for a while after it has been built. Some of these problems can be more severe than others. If the foundation was laid on land that was not properly prepared, the settling problems can be dangerous.

Some cracks that appear in masonry walls near doors in windows are not necessarily the result of settling; they could result from the effect of expansion and contraction of surrounding wood structures during seasonal changes. These cracks are best filled with a material that will give a little, because there is really no way of stopping the expansion and contraction of the surrounding wood. Perhaps the best material to use is one of the vinyl caulking compounds. This material will harden enough to make a leak-tight joint, but it will remain flexible enough to compensate for the expansion and contraction of the wood.

Whether the crack is in a poured concrete wall, one made of bricks and mortar, or of construction block, the repair steps are pretty much the same. But, before you undertake the repairs, it would be wise to determine if the settling is still going on. If so, it is usually better to wait until it has gone as far as it will.

You can determine if settling is still taking place by applying a small patch of plaster across the crack. If there is still movement, the plaster will crack. Wait a few months and if the plaster test patch doesn't crack, it's safe to proceed with the patching work. This may seem like a long time to wait, but it's best to be sure.

If you have such a condition, it would be wise to seek the advice of a professional; the work needed may be more than just the filling of a crack. Steps may have to be taken to solve the cause of the settling first.

If the crack is long and deep and runs through the brick as well as the mortar joints, you will want to be sure that the entire crack is filled. Just covering the crack with some mortar will keep it from being seen, but a structural repair is really required and this means that you will have to fill the entire crack.

A proper mixture of mortar will not flow into the crack,

so you will have to use grout. Grout is a thin mixture that is used mainly for tile work, but it is ideal for the job of filling a big crack. Rather than blend your own, it's best to get a package of pre-mixed grout and mix it with water according to the instructions on the package.

You will want to get the grout all the way into the crack and this is difficult with conventional tools. You can use a piece of plastic tubing used to supply air to a fish tank, and connect it to the spout of a funnel. Feed the tube into the top of the crack as far as possible and then begin to pour the grout into the funnel. The inside of the crack should be thoroughly dampened first.

To prevent the grout from running out of the crack as it is filled up, you can temporarily seal the crack with masking

9-4
Here's how to get thin grout to fill a crack completely.

tape. When the grout hardens, the tape can be peeled away.

If you have a big crack, it is often advisable to fill it in several stages. Fill the lower portion first, and when it has hardened, repeat the process until you have repaired the entire crack.

If you are repairing a crack that runs through bricks as well as mortar joints, the patch will be obvious in the brick. But you can solve this problem by working a mortar color that matches the color of the brick into the grout before it fully hardens. Or you can wait until it is fully hardened and then rub a scrap of old brick over the mortar. The color of the brick will wear off on the mortar.

HOW TO REPLACE DAMAGED BRICK

Brick is a porous building material. When it rains, brick will take up considerable quantities of moisture. If this occurs before cold weather, the moisture in the brick may freeze and the resulting expansion can cause cracks.

Whenever it becomes necessary to replace a brick, it can be done by following these steps. First, chip out all of the mortar that surrounds the brick. Use a sharpened cold chisel and a hammer to do the job. Be careful that you don't damage any of the surrounding brick. After all of the mortar has been chipped free, a few taps on the damaged brick should be enough to loosen it so that it can be slid out.

With the damaged brick removed, chisel away any remaining mortar in the cavity and then clean it thoroughly with a wire brush. After the wire brushing, use a brush such as a whisk broom to clear away all the debris and dust.

Be sure that you have an appropriate replacement brick, and proceed by mixing enough fresh mortar to seal the new brick in place. Wet down the surfaces in the cavity and the replacement brick. The surfaces should be damp but have no standing water.

Apply the mortar to the bottom of the cavity; lay enough so that when the brick is positioned in place, it will follow the line of the surrounding bricks. Wet the new brick and place it on the bed of mortar. Jiggle the brick slightly to make sure it makes firm contact with the mortar.

With the brick positioned, begin to force fresh mortar in around it with the trowel. As you work the mortar in, jiggle the trowel ever so slightly. This will cause the mortar to settle, and reduce the possibility of bubbles. When you have filled the area surrounding the brick with mortar, use the trowel to point the mortar in the same style as the rest of the brickwork.

If the cause of the cracking was moisture freezing within the brick, you can solve this problem by applying a coat of clear brick sealer to the surface. Be sure to wait for the mortar to dry and apply the sealer to the entire brick area—to all of the bricks and mortar.

HOW TO HANDLE THE PROBLEM OF EFFLORESCENCE

Efflorescence is a whitish, powdery substance that often can be seen on the surface of a masonry wall. It is actually crystallized water-soluble salts that have been washed to the surface of the wall. It's not a problem in itself, but it is an indicator of other problems.

Efflorescence requires water to make it appear. If the water is coming from the other side of a cellar wall, you should investigate the problem and take steps to correct it. Such steps often require that the dirt be removed from the outside of the cellar wall and that some rather elaborate water-proofing steps be taken to prevent further penetration. You can do this by yourself; the job of waterproofing is not especially difficult, but the job of trenching around the foundation is the big problem. However, if you decide to undertake the job, get the advice of an expert first. A number of conditions can exist, both in the surrounding earth as well as in the wall, so that any specific instructions at this point would not be very helpful.

To solve the efflorescence problem on the wall, first use a stiff wire brush to remove all of the powdery crystals. To do a complete job, dip the brush in a solution made of one part muriatic acid and ten parts water. This solution is harmful; wear rubber gloves and safety glasses, and don't splash it on clothing. After scrubbing with the acid solution, flush the surface with fresh water.

HOW TO REPAIR DAMAGED CONCRETE WALLS

A concrete walk or driveway can become damaged just from use as a car is driven over it regularly. It can settle because the earth beneath it was poorly prepared before the drive was poured, and it can suffer badly from frost and freezing effects.

Whatever the cause of the problem, if it is small enough, it is better to use one of the epoxy materials to fill in the crack. You can also buy patching material made of other plastic compounds that will work just as well. Be sure to follow the instructions on the particular material you select.

If the crack is too large for such measures, it should be repaired with a pre-mixed gravel mix, or you can make a patching material by mixing one part portland cement, two parts sand and two parts fine gravel. Add only enough water to make a stiff mix.

Before any of the patching material is applied, you should use a chisel to chip away all thin edges and to undercut both sides of the crack to insure a tight grip for the patch. You should also roughen up the inside of the crack with the chisel.

Use a stiff wire brush to clean the crack of loose debris, and then go over the crack again with a stiff brush, such as a

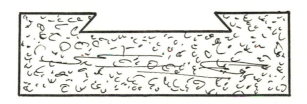

9-5
An undercut insures that a concrete patch will hold firmly in place.

whisk broom. Wet the crack and the surrounding concrete thoroughly, but be sure that there is no standing water before you pour in the mixed concrete. Tamp the mixture thoroughly in the crack; a 2 × 4 can be used to do this, but be sure that it is thoroughly soaked so that it doesn't draw moisture from the mix.

Overfill the crack slightly to accommodate any shrinkage that will take place. Smooth the surface with a trowel, or use a scrap of dampened wood.

Be sure to let the patch cure for six or seven days before the walk is put back in service. Spray the patch and the surrounding concrete occasionally with a light mist to prevent improper curing.

HOW TO REPAIR A DAMAGED CONCRETE STEP

If the steps are cracked on the surface of the tread or riser, follow the steps just outlined to take care of the problem; but if it is the edge that is crumbling or broken, the problem can be solved in the following way.

Use a hammer and cold chisel to chip away all loose and crumbling concrete. The chances are that the opening you will have made will be somewhat jagged and uneven. You will have to cut into the solid concrete to try to get an even edge on the tread and riser and you should try to cut back into the step to get a V-shaped undercut in the tread. An undercut will help strengthen the patch.

Once you have made the undercut, clear away all of the debris and locate a board that will cover the width of the step. This board is to serve as a form to hold the poured mortar in place as it cures. Position the board snugly against the riser; it can be held in place with a wooden bracket or any heavy object.

Because most damaged step edges seldom require a lot of mortar, it's best to buy pre-mixed material to do the job. Mix it according to the instructions, but before you apply it, the

9-6-A
The edges are usually the first to go.

9-6-B
Chisel out the damaged area to provide a firm grip
for fresh mortar.

9-6-C
Place a board against the step to retain the fresh mortar.
Brace the form with blocks or heavy stones.
Pour the fresh mortar.

opened step edge and surrounding concrete should be wet down thoroughly.

Work a little of the mortar into the crack, covering the entire surface. You can work it in with your fingers or use a trowel. This will help make a tight bond with the step. Next, pour in enough mortar to fill the opened area to the level of the tread. The board will hold the mortar in place to form a continuation of the riser when it is dry. You might want to overpour ever so slightly to accommodate for shrinkage when the mortar dries.

A step patch such as this should be left to cure for six or seven days before the steps put back in use. To cure, you can cover the new material with dampened burlap, or apply a light spray from a garden hose often enough to keep the patch and the surrounding concrete damp. Don't flood the area.

HOW TO SEAL A BLACKTOP DRIVEWAY

Sealers are applied to tar driveways to protect the surface from snow, water and the sun. The sealer is a black, gloppy substance and it is most often sold in five-gallon cans. Five gallons are enough to coat about 250 square feet. Be sure to compute the area of your drive before you buy the sealer; it's no fun to start the job on Sunday—when the stores are often closed—and find that you don't have sufficient material.

Before you do the job of sealing, be sure that the drive-

9-7
An old push broom is an ideal tool to spread blacktop sealer.

way has been swept clean of everything, not just the kids' toys and some loose gravel. Any dust and grime will make it difficult for the sealer to adhere to the surface.

Once the driveway is clean, pour a small amount of the sealer at one end of the driveway and begin to work it in with an old push broom. When you have spread it as far as it can go, pour down some more and continue until you have finished.

Don't lay the sealer down in too thick a layer. It's best to apply two thin coats, two days apart, rather than to apply one thicker coating. It takes more work, but the extra effort will be well worth it. The two-coat surface will be much more durable than a single, thicker coating.

HOW TO PATCH CRACKS IN BLACKTOP

Temperature changes, wearing conditions and a shifting ground beneath the driveway can all contribute to the problem of cracking.

Small cracks in blacktop can be filled directly with the same material that is used as a sealer. But, if you have some larger cracks, you can do a first-class job of repair with a mix

9-8
Cracks can be patched with a mixture of sand and blacktop sealer.

of the sealer and some clean sand. The mixture should be stiff but workable. Use a trowel or a small garden hand spade to work the mixture into the crack. Pack it in tightly and smooth off the surface. If the surface settles after a while, just add more of the mixture.

Finish the repair by dusting the surface of the patch with some fine sand. The sand will become embedded in the surface and give the patch additional wearing ability.

HOW TO FILL A HOLE IN BLACKTOP

When the driveway is made, it's usually one of the last things a contractor does before he turns over the keys to a new home owner. All during the construction of the house, scraps of wood from cutting and trimming find their way into the ground all around the house. If the builder is not careful to remove the wood before a blacktop driveway is made, there is a good chance that holes will develop in the driveway in years to come.

As the wood decomposes, it leaves a pocket and the driveway sinks to fill the void. When the sinking is severe enough, the edges of the pocket will break and there will often be a significant hole in the driveway. Of course, holes can develop by other means, but the rotting wood is often respon-

9-9-A
Remove all the loose blacktop and chip away the soft edges.

sible for holes that seem to get deeper and deeper until they look like miniature craters.

To fill these holes, and holes formed by any other means, you should begin by using a spade to break in the edges until you are on solid ground. Then, scoop out all of the material in the hole, and if you can, dig into the earth below to get at the rotting wood.

9-9-B
Partially fill the hole with coarse gravel.

Holes in blacktop are best filled with a material that is made specially for the job; it's a cold-mix patching compound that is sold in 66 pound paper bags. Feel the bag to make sure that it is loose and workable before you buy it. If the bag has been stored in the cold, it may feel solid only because of the

9-9-C
Fill the hole with blacktop patching material.

temperature. When warmed up, it might be loose enough to work.

Before any of the patching material is put in the hole, fill it with coarse gravel to within two or three inches of the top. Use the end of a 2 × 4 or a 4 × 4 to tamp this gravel firmly in position. Now, you are ready to add some cold-mix asphalt patching material. Put in enough so that it is about an inch

9-9-D
Tamp the patch. Add more patching material and tamp,
if necessary.

from the top of the hole. Use the wood to tamp the material vigorously. When you feel that you cannot compress the material any more, add enough to reach the top of the hole. Tamp this again. Continue adding patching material until it is level with the edge of the hole.

This material is sticky. You can help prevent it from being tracked into the house by wiping a coat of coarse sand over the finished patch.

For a final packing, drive your car over it several times.

INDEX

A

Aluminum
  gutters, 68-71
  painting, 137
  screens, 176-178
Asbestos, shingles, repairing, 110
  walls, painting, 137
Asphalt, *see* blacktop

B

Blacktop
  filling holes, 234-236
  patching, 233-234
Brick
  cracked, 16
  replacing, 227-228
  repointing, 222-224
Brushes
  care, 134-136
  choosing, 132-134
  dusting, 133
  flat, 133
  masonry, 133
  sash, 133
  trim, 133
  wire, 128

C

Caulking
  aluminized, 54
  butyl, 54

Caulking *(cont'd.)*
  latex, 101
  leaks, 98
  oil base, 100-101
  rope, 100
  silicone, 100
  surface preparation, 102-103
  polyvinyl acetate, 101
Cement, asphalt, 54
  see mortar
Chimney
  cap, 92-93
  cleaning, 78-80
  construction, 77
  fireplace, 93
  flashing, 83-89
  keeping rain out, 82-83
  leaning, 89
  loose brick, 91-92
  mortar replacement, 90-91
  problem check-list, 19
  rain problems, 82-83
  smoke leaks, 89-90
  spark arrester, 81-82
Concrete, using, 220-222

D

Doors
  garage, 211-213
  hinge mortise, deepening, 184-185
  hinge, screw hole repair, 182-183
  hinge shim, installing, 183-184
  latch, repairing, 189-191

Doors *(cont'd.)*
    peepholes, installing, 195-196
    problem check-list, 21
    removing, 185-186
    saddle, replacing, 193-195
    sliding, repairing, 200-202
    sticking, 186-189
    warped, 191-192
    weatherstripping, 197-200
Downspout
    cleaning, 58-59
    problem check-list, 18
Driveway
    blacktop, sealing, 232-233
    blacktop, holes, filling, 234-235
    blacktop, patching cracks, 233-234
    problem check-list, 21
Drywell, installation, 72-74

E

Efflorescense, curing, 228–229

F

Finishes, problem check-list, 20
Fireplace, problems, 93
Flashing
    exterior joints, 53
    chimney, repairing, 83-85
    chimney, replacing, 85-89
    closed and open valley, 51-52
    repairing, 48-49
    vent-pipe, replacing, 49-51
Foundation, repairing, 224-227

G

Garage door
    leaks, 212-213
    rot, 212-213
    track repairs, 211-212
Glass
    aluminum windows, 169-170
    casement windows, 165-166

Glass *(cont'd.)*
    cutting, 160-161
    jalousie windows, 170-171
    replacing, 156-159
    storm windows, 168-169
Gutters
    aluminum, installation, 69-71
    aluminum, maintenance, 68-69
    cleaning, 58
    copper, 68
    dry wall connection, 72-74
    installation, 69-71
    leaf guards, 59-61
    patching, large holes, 66
    patching, small holes, 63-66
    plastic, 69
    problem check-list, 18
    sagging, 61-63
    snow guards, 74
    steel, 67-68
    strainers, 59-61
    wood, 66-67

H

Hinges, 182-185

J

Joints
    caulking, 97-102
    leaking, 99-100

K

Key
    broken, 204-205
    failure, 206
    frozen, 205
    jammed, 205

L

Ladder, extension, 27-31
Latchbolt, adjusting, 206

Leafguards, installing, 59-61
Leaks, locating, 31-33
Locks
    bolt, jammed, 206
    key, broken, 204-205
    key, failure, 206
    key, jammed, 205
    mortise, 209-211
    problem check-list, 21
    sticking, 203-204
    unfreezing, 205
    tubular, cylinder, 206-209

M

Mildew, eliminating, 114-116
Mortar
    coloring, 219
    mixing, 218-219
    using, 220

O

Oakum, use with caulking, 103

P

Painting
    alligatoring, 122-123
    blisters, 5, 119-120
    brushes, 132-136
    brush care, 134-136
    caulking, 129-130
    checking, 122-123
    chemical removal, 127-128
    choosing paint, 137-138
    crawling, 123
    decks, 141-142
    discoloration, 124
    efflorescense, 125-126
    gutters, 140-141
    heat removal, 126-127
    mildew, 124-125
    moss, 125
    order of application, 139
    peeling, 121-122

Painting (cont'd.)
    porches, 141-142
    problems, 119-126
    runs, 124
    sags, 124
    sandpapering, 129
    siding, 140
    slow drying, 121
    staining, 131-132
    surface preparation, 126-132
    washing, 130-131
    wire brushing, 128
    wrinkling, 123-124

R

Repointing brick, 222-224
Roof
    asphalt shingles, repairing, 33-34
    asphalt shingles, replacing, 34-36
    ceramic tile, 45-48
    flashing, repairing, 48-53
    hip shingles, repairing, 36
    hip shingles, replacing, 37-38
    painting, 39
    patching, 40-44
    patching materials, 54
    problem check-list, 17
    slate shingles, repairing, 38
    slate shingles, replacing, 38-39
    wood shingles, repairing, 44
    wood shingles, replacing, 45

S

Safety, 22
Sandpaper, 129
Sash balance, 154-155
Sash cord, 149-154
Screens
    aluminum, 176-178
    gashed, 175
    maintenance, 172-173
    patching large holes, 173-174
    patching small holes, 173
    plastic, 175
    problem check-list, 20
    seasonal problems, 22
    wood frame, 175-176

Shingles
    asbestos, replacing, 110
    asphalt, repairing, 33
    asphalt, replacing, 34-36
    slate, repairing, 38
    slate, replacing, 38-39
    hip, repairing, 36
    hip, replacing, 37
    wood, repairing, 44
    wood, replacing, 45, 109-110
    wood, warped, 108
Siding
    asbestos shingles, replacing, 110
    caulking gun use, 103
    caulking joints, 97-101
    caulking, surface preparation, 102-103
    caulking, types, 100-101
    clapboard, replacing, 106-108
    clapboard, split, 104-105
    clapboard, warped, 104
    mildew, 115-117
    problem check-list, 19
    stucco, mixing, 111
    stucco, patching small cracks, 111-112
    stucco, patching large holes, 112-113
    stucco, patching holes on block wall, 113-114
    wood shingles, replacing, 109-110
    wood shingles, warped, 108
Skylight, leaks, 53
Sleeve and spike support, 62
Snow guards, installing, 74
Spark arrester, installing, 81-82
Splashblocks, installing, 71-72
Steps, concrete, repairing, 230-232
Storm windows
    condensation, 167-168
    problem check-list, 20
    replacing glass, 168-169
Stoves, wood burning, 79
Strainers, leaf, 59-61
Stucco
    mixing, 111
    patching large holes, 112-113
    patching on concrete walls, 113-114
    patching small cracks, 111-112

T

Trowel, using, 220-221

V

Vent pipe, flashing, 49-51

W

Walks
    repairing, 217-222
    problem check-list, 21
Walls
    brick, replacing, 227-228
    brick, repointing, 222-224
    concrete, repairing, 229-230
    problem check-list, 21
Windows
    aluminum, replacing glass, 169-170
    awning, 172
    casement, description, 163-164
    casement, lubricating, 164-165
    casement, replacing glass, 165-166
    casement, weatherstripping, 165
    double-hung, description, 146-147
    double-hung, lubricating, 149
    double-hung, sticking, 147-149
    double-hung, weatherstripping, 161-163
    glass, cutting, 160-161
    jalousie, description, 170
    jalousie, replacing glass, 170-171
    jalousie, leaks, 170
    jalousie, lubricating, 171
    jalousie, maintenance, 171
    problem checklist, 20
    sashcord, replacing, 149-154
    sash balance, installing, 154-155
    spring-lift, adjusting, 155-156
    storm, description, 166-167
    storm, condensation, 167-168
    storm, replacing glass, 168-169
    storm, reinforcing, 168-169
    wood, replacing glass, 156-160
Wire brush, 128

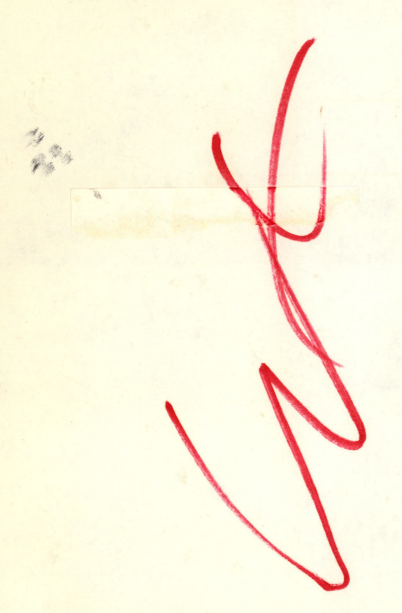